PERFORMANCE MEASURES
FOR PUBLIC LIBRARIES

Ernest R. De Prospo   Ellen Altman
Kenneth E. Beasley

with the assistance of

Ellen C. Clark

D1451718

PUBLIC LIBRARY ASSOCIATION
AMERICAN LIBRARY ASSOCIATION

Sponsored by the American Library Association

Funded by the U.S. Office of Education
  Bureau of Libraries and Educational Technology

Library of Congress Cataloging in Publication Data

De Prospo, Ernest R   1937-
    Performance measures for public libraries.

    Report by the staff of the project on the first
three phases of the Measurement and Effectiveness of
Public Library Service Study, sponsored by the Public
Library Association and conducted by the Bureau of
Library and Information Sciences Research, Rutgers
University.
    Includes bibliographical references.
    1. Public libraries--United States--Statistics.
2. Public libraries--United States--Evaluation.
I. Altman, Ellen, joint author. II. Beasley, Kenneth
E., joint author. III. Measurement and Effectiveness
of Public Library Service Study. IV. Public Library
Association. V. Title.
Z731.D45   027.4'0973   73-16427
ISBN 0-8389-3149-9

Printed in the United States of America

Second Printing, 1974

Project Advisory Committee:

> Frank B. Sessa, Graduate School of Library and Information
> Sciences, University of Pittsburgh, Chairman
> Forest R. Carhart, Jr., New York Metropolitan Reference and
> Research Library Agency (METRO)
> Walter W. Curley, Cleveland Public Library
> Phyllis I. Dalton, formerly California State Library
> Eleanor A. Ferguson, New York State Library
> John C. Frantz, National Book Committee
> Harold Goldstein, Library School, Florida State University
> Mary E. Phillips, formerly Library Association of Portland, Oregon
> Gerald M. Born, Executive Secretary, Public Library Association,
> ALA Liaison

Project Staff:

> Kenneth E. Beasley, Principal Investigator
> Ernest R. De Prospo, Project Director
> Ellen Altman, Research Associate
> Ellen C. Clark, Research Assistant

Acknowledgements

Although it is impossible to mention all of the individuals who contributed to this study, we would like to acknowledge our debt to those who gave us special assistance. Our ALA Advisory Committee offered us their counsel and support for two years. Philip Clark, Ralph Blasingame and Henry Voos freely served as sounding boards for all our ideas. Jewel Walton spent many hours collecting data in the pilot libraries and gave us insights from the practicing librarian's viewpoint. Two of our students, the late Harold Gray of Rutgers and Judith Hist of Kentucky worked many tedious hours coding data as did Randall Yoneshige. Ann Mullin not only typed and re-typed the manuscripts but also edited the final draft. Gerald M. Born, Executive Secretary of PLA, took care of the myriad administrative duties connected with the project and this publication. Most of all, we thank the directors and staffs of the participating libraries for their support and enthusiasm.

CONTENTS

Introduction

This document has been prepared in response to the many inquiries for information concerning progress on the Measurement of Effectiveness of Public Library Service Study. Although only the first three phases of the project have been funded and completed, the Public Library Association Board and the research team felt that enough significant findings have emerged to make their dissemination worthwhile. It should be kept in mind that this document is preliminary in nature and that it is the intent of the Public Library Association and the research team to further test and refine the study as funds become available.

The Study addresses problems that have occupied the library world for the last two decades. As a result of the 1956 Public Library Standards, a need to measure the service capabilities of the public library became evident. Traditional measures, such as circulation, did not suffice to give an accurate picture of the use made of the public library nor of its benefit to the community. New measures recognizing the satisfaction of the user and a more adequate evaluation of library service were needed.

The Study grew out of the accreditation project of the Public Library Association which was rewritten in 1967 and submitted to the ALA Executive Board, for its approval at that time. The first two phases of the project were approved and funded by the U.S. Office of Education in 1970. Final authorization was obtained in 1971. Sufficient funds were not available to undertake the entire project at that time, but it had been designed in such a way that if additional funds were not granted for future phases the project would still be viable to that particular stage.

The Study was sponsored by the Public Library Association under the auspices of the American Library Association and was conducted by the Bureau of Library and Information Science Research at Rutgers University. Dr. Kenneth Beasley, Dean, The Graduate School, University of Texas at El Paso, was named as Principal Investigator and Dr. Ernest R. DeProspo, Professor, Graduate School of Library Service, Rutgers University, named as Project Director. Dr. Ellen Altman, currently Assistant Professor, University of Kentucky was Research Associate, and Mrs. Ellen Clark of Rutgers University, was Research Assistant. As work progressed on the project, it was evaluated at various stages by an Advisory Committee appointed by the Public Library Association. The Advisory Committee's input helped formulate and determine the direction of the project, and from time to time modified and corrected its course. This document is intended to be used by anyone, public librarian, trustee, or interested party, as a background for the study of measurement techniques as applied to public libraries and to illustrate the thinking that led to the indicators found to be effective discriminators of public library service. The Study, based on a sound research methodology, opens the door to new

ways of gathering library statistics and applying them to decision making. The purpose of this study is to find new ways of describing library service in statistical terms and creating a better profile of
library operation than has been possible in the past. Certain criteria
were kept constantly in mind: The technique had to be relatively
simple; data had to be gathered in a relatively short period of time by
the library staff, not trained researchers. It was also necessary to be
able to use information that was easily gathered and available in public
libraries.

The data generated by the project enable the preparation of a much
different profile of public libraries than has ever been possible to
construct. It shows, by use of sampling techniques, the character of
the collection, the use of the facility and the characteristics of users
as well as providing information on the outreach services offered by the
public library. Armed with such information, the administrator should
be able to make more judicious use of time and materials and have a
factual basis on which to plan and make budget allocation. The Study,
insofar as it has charted new courses on largely unknown waters, may be
viewed as a pioneer work. As more detailed information becomes available, it is conceivable that other measures and indicators will be found
that will enable librarians to formulate sophisticated and specific data
about the operation and efficiency of their library.

                                   Gerald M. Born
                                   Executive Secretary
                                   Public Library Association

1. Observations on Measurement

Public libraries in the U.S. had a total income in 1970 of $743,227,127.[1] Since the growth in income for nearly two decades has been steady and has come almost entirely from tax appropriations, increasing concern has developed about the benefits accruing from public library service. The point has now been reached where traditional arguments for public support of expanded service are not as meaningful as in the past, and do not evoke as strong an emotional response. Indeed, a negative reaction could develop if strong popular pressures demanded a higher priority for certain other social services.

Such a trend already appears to be emerging as libraries are being forced to compete with other vital public services for revenue sharing funds. Also, the present inflationary spiral has driven costs to unprecedented levels. As a result, budget officials are less and less willing to accept the values of library service on faith alone and are pressing for accountability in terms of performance measures.

Yet, attempts at measuring library services generally, and public library services, specifically, are seriously handicapped or nullified by the continual rejection of their usefulness by the librarian "under fire." The approaches have been seen as too esoteric or too complicated or too remote from reality or too simplistic or too narrow or too broad or too . . . . On the other hand, the researcher has too often worked in a vacuum, not sufficiently sensitized to the world of library operations to make the crucial connection between methodology and meaning of importance. Or, the marriage between researcher and practitioner has been so close that objectivity is impossible. In general, there has been an absence of adequate transmittal of knowledge from the techniques used by researchers to the practitioners responsible for their final interpretation and implementation.

Clearly, if the researcher's interest goes beyond insight into the problem of "how" to measure and includes the concern of acceptance and utilization of the given scheme developed, then an understanding of the "politics" of measurement is essential. While the politics of measurement are multi-dimensional, two stand out in their importance. First, there are the pressures from outside agents such as local budget officers, city managers and other local bureaucrats, to conform to devices which they, the agents, have devised as reliable indicators of performance. Second, there is the general skepticism about any statistical approach which purports to measure quality. The ambivalence of the profession towards library statistics, despite or because of its historical antecedents, has helped to create a vacuum today which explains the dilemma in which most library decision-makers find themselves.

1

The rejection of suggested statistical reporting systems or approaches--
rejection in terms of behavior not necessarily the verbiage--is forcing
the library decision-maker to accept the outside agents' "tools" as
adequate substitutes. And, the library decision-maker appears to be
generally unhappy with the results so far. More importantly, the profession is clearly in no stronger power position as a result.

In our view, those researchers who have dealt with the problem of
statistical measurement have not done a very good job in communicating
their schemes to those under operational fire. They have not proved the
case for either the relevance or operational meaning of the approaches
devised. They have tended to act as if the world of statistical measurement is crystal clear to everyone; its meaning instantly obvious. They
have ignored then, the "politics of measurement."

Perhaps C. West Churchman is correct when he concludes in his book
that "ultimate meaning of the systems approach,...lies in the creation
of a theory of deception and in a fuller understanding of the ways in
which the human being can be deceived about his world and in an interaction between these different viewpoints."[2]

The thrust of Churchman's argument is that the planner or researcher has not really faced up to the multiple factors, rational or irra-
tional, which significantly undermine his schemes. "...among the anti-
planners there is the completely non-intellectual approach, the approach
that does not believe that thinking in any of its senses is important
in the development of human life."[3]

We suppose one would encounter a more receptive group if a total
condemnation of statistics and the prospect of relating quality with
quantity prefaced all ensuing comments. We could then conclude that
despite its inherent weakness the statistical approach would clearly be
the lesser evil and should be given a try. At the very least, we guess,
we would have made our contribution towards the art of deception. The
unfortunate case is the prevalent confusion between the abuses of the
technique with the logical foundation of its existence. Rationally
we know that quantity infers something about quality--a reading room
with one seat or a library with one book suggests certain limitations
on the quality of those operations! Emotionally, of course, we resist
any such connection. And too often it is just that emotion which deter-
mines our behavior in the final analysis.

The notion of "measurement" is one which tends to exacerbate an
already complex set of circumstances. The multiple views and long
standing doubts over the meaning and use of this term often get in the
way of methodology. It is important, therefore, to state briefly the
views of the research team on "measurement" and the values which were
brought to this study.

Too often numbers or statistics are treated as having an intrinsic
scientific value, so powerful that using them is often seen as an end in
itself. Just as the overemphasis on definitions often approaches a faith
in the power of the word, so too the mystique of quantity is often an
exaggerated regard for the significance of measurement, just because it
is quantitative, without regard for what has been measured or what can
subsequently be done with the measure. What is really important is
how one can become more sure of what he thinks he already knows.

Although measurement is by no means the only method of extending or solidifying our knowledge, clearly it has an important role to play in this understanding process.

Measurement serves as a key device for standardization, a process through which we are convinced of equivalences among varied objects. As such, measurement allows subtle discriminations and, correspondingly, more precise descriptions. Such quantitative specification allows us to bring our differing professional disagreements into a sharper and more illuminating focus. In the final analysis, however, it should be remembered that whether one can measure something is dependent on how one is able to conceptualize about the things to be measured. Conceptualization is dependent on our knowledge of the things to be measured and, most importantly, on the skill and ingenuity which is brought to bear on the process. The following pages will outline our attempt to assess the performance of public libraries.

Outline of the Study

In 1971, the U.S. Office of Education authorized a study to develop criteria to measure the effectiveness of public libraries. This project was sponsored by the American Library Association and conducted by the Bureau of Library and Information Science Research at Rutgers University. The basic rationale for this study was simply put in the proposal.

Attempts to measure the service capabilities of public libraries, either in relation to the needs of their communities or to the standards adopted by the profession, are hampered by the lack of criteria of quality or effectiveness. [New measures are needed which]...must gauge effectiveness while eliminating extraneous factors. The required data must be such that library staffs can collect them with a reasonable expenditure of time. Some investigators have suggested such measures, but have not taken the second step proposed here of matching the results against objective professional judgments of effectiveness.[4]

The project as originally structured contained five distinct phases as outlined below.

Phase I

1. Reviewing previous efforts to assess effectiveness of library service as reported in the literature.
2. Analyzing present library statistical reporting systems and their applicability as indicators of effectiveness.

Phase II

1. Developing criteria which appear descriptive of the effectiveness of a public library program.
2. Developing a methodology for the data collection process for the selected criteria.
3. Collecting data in a small number of pilot libraries to test the feasibility of the method.
4. Establishing tentative ranges of performance for each criterion.

Phase III
    1. Testing the criteria and methodology developed during Phase
       I in a sample of public libraries on a nationwide basis.
    2. Preparation of a "profile" for each of the sample libraries.
Phase IV
    1. On-site visitations of some of the Phase II libraries to
       determine to what extent the measurement indicators developed
       coincide with professional judgment about the effectiveness
       of service provided by those libraries.
Phase V
    1. Detailed analysis and summary report.

Only Phases I through III have been funded to date and the availability of further funding to complete the study appears doubtful. However, we have received so many requests for information about this project during the past two years, that we decided to share the information available at this point with the profession.

Please keep in mind that our findings are preliminary. Until support for detailed analysis is available we cannot offer final conclusions.

A few caveats are in order. It is important to state what the study is not and to describe the considerations which have imposed constraints on the study. The especially strong "humanistic" strain which runs through the profession requires that open and honest consideration be given to the emotional and intellectual factors which approaches at "measurement," "evaluation," "quantification," present. For many librarians the doubt that one can infer quality from quantity is sufficiently strong that any method which asserts, per se, that numbers will provide the basis for professional consensus on what constitutes "acceptable levels of performance" runs the likely risk of outright rejection.

Obviously, not all library activities are subject to reasonable quantification or objective verification. Furthermore, numerous library activities take place which are considered valuable to "society" but not particularly as efficient or measurable as such, for example, the time a librarian spends with a senior citizen. While the study to date shows more clearly than past writings what some of the limitations are in quantification, this work should be viewed as a first step effort on a macro level at identifying some important common "core" library activities which are amenable to quantification.

Obviously, all one can hope to accomplish with this preliminary effort is to identify some of the public library "norms" which characterize their basic operations. In so doing we should be capable of pointing out both similarities and differences, particularly as they relate to the size of the public library operation. And, as with any "norm," we would expect deviations in either direction. To the extent that these norms accurately describe public library operations, we should be able to identify major implications for broad-based library policy. Refinement which gets at detailed and specific analysis, or micro level analysis, must await further study.

NOTES

1/ R.R. Bowker, Inc., The Bowker Annual of Library and Book Trade Information, 1971 (Bowker, 1971), pp. 50-1.

2/ C. West Churchman, The Systems Approach (Dell, 1968), pp. 229-30.

3/ Ibid., p. 225.

4/ Kenneth E. Beasley, Measurement of Effectiveness of Public Library Service. Proposal for Research Submitted to the U.S. Commissioner of Education. January, 1970.

2. Research on Library Performance

The literature is replete with articles entitled: "Evaluation of Library Services," "Measurements in Library Service," "Quality Values of Library Service," "Indices of Effectiveness of Public Library Services," "Measurement and Evaluation," "Evaluation of Library Services in Depth." Unfortunately, none of these authors fulfilled the promise offered by their titles. They offered no formulae but simply exhortations to strive for effectiveness or to use techniques which have been proven unsatisfactory from past experience. All of these titles refer to public libraries. Publications dealing with special and university libraries have their share of this type of article too. However, some innovative work has been done in special and university libraries, much of it by persons outside librarianship.

Some of the most important studies have utilized two techniques borrowed from industry and military organizations. These are systems analysis and operations research, both of which rely heavily on statistical methods. Systems analysis is a functional process which segregates and delineates the individual functions of an organization. It shows the interfaces between functions and their relationship to overall objectives. Operations research uses a systems orientation based on the idea that the activity of any part of an organization has some effect on the activity of every other part. Therefore, it is necessary to identify all significant interactions and to evaluate their combined impact on organizational performance as a whole. This involves the development of mathematical models and simulations of various subsystems.

Because some library operations lend themselves readily to quantification and hence are amenable to the construction of models, these areas have been prime targets for investigation by researchers. For example, weeding, storage and duplication have been analyzed again and again, most notably by Trueswell,[1] Fussler and Simon,[2] and Jain.[3] They essentially view the library as an inventory supply problem and try to assess which materials will be called for most frequently and which will languish on the shelves. All have found that the probability of a book's being used declines with its age. This finding, in turn, relates to Trueswell's 80/20 rule which says that 20 percent of a university library's collection accounts for 80 percent of its outside circulation.[4] The 80/20 rule may not apply to public libraries because of the large percentage of fiction in their collections.

Another group of studies has attempted to analyze a variety of library activities by employing sophisticated mathematical techniques. Philip M. Morse's book Library Effectiveness applies operations research techniques to a variety of library activities. Morse's criteria of performance is "unsatisfied document demand." As a result, the book focuses primarily on book use and its implications for satisfying both current and future demands for material. He shows the interaction of demand to circulation, weeding, and duplication.[5]

The models developed in the book can be used as a data base for decision-making at the Massachusetts Institute of Technology Science Library. The formulas could be adapted to other libraries once preliminary data had been collected. A major advantage of Morse's method is that the models can be updated without gathering much additional data because they are based on probabilistic occurances. In fact, it would be possible to re-study only selected areas of a library's operation once the initial data have been collected.

A serious problem with this study is its lack of intelligibility to the average practicing librarian. The writing style and method of presentation make no concessions to those unfamiliar with statistical terminology and notation. A library wishing to utilize these formulae would probably have to employ a statistician or an operations researcher to analyze and interpret the data.

Another sophisticated study was Wessel's attempt to develop criteria to evaluate the efficiency and effectiveness of Army technical library operations and services.[6] Operations were defined as practical tasks resulting in a product for internal use of the library. Acquisitions and cataloging are examples of operations. Services include literature searching, abstracting and indexing.

Since the study focused on development of criteria for assessing efficiency and effectiveness, the first phase of the work attempted to discover existing criteria either in library literature or in use in these Army libraries. The second phase analyzed the "mission" statements (goals) of these libraries and their parent organizations to determine if any patterns existed which could be used as a base for the establishment of "candidate" criteria. The candidate criteria fell into four general categories.

1. Philosophical--reasons for the existence of the library and the purposes which it serves.
2. Management--administrative effectiveness.
3. Services--characteristics and value of outputs.
4. Operations--daily routines involved in running the library.

The management experts on the research team identified about 50 specific management techniques which had potential application to libraries. These techniques were grouped under the following broad categories:

1. Systems analysis
2. Cost effectiveness
3. Operations research
4. Charting
5. Operations analysis
6. Procurement inventory study
7. Personnel administration
8. Economics
9. Planning
10. Information theory
11. Control

12. Plant layout analysis
13. Organization analysis
14. Management appraisal

Each technique was evaluated against all others for each library function. A matrix was constructed showing the most appropriate technique for each function and indicating whether this technique could be used as an "indicator of effectiveness," an "indicator of efficiency" or a "controller of performance."

Phase III involved correlation tests of library statistics to explore the possible relationships between these statistics and efficiency and effectiveness. The purpose of the tests was to develop normative standards. Many of these correlations were related to work load and costs.

A utility analysis approach required the library directors to assign weights or values to the operations and services performed in the library in relation to the overall mission of the library. The idea was to establish criteria for the allocation of man hours to maximize the utility of operations and services. Mathematical models were presented to illustrate what changes in output might result by altering the "utility" value of the service or operation.

The models are well-conceived and theoretically sound. However, actually applying them might prove difficult since as the authors note "...the librarians are often not able to quantify the values of operations in supporting services or values of operations in supporting mission."[7] This difficulty would probably be compounded in public libraries since there is a paucity of data on unit costs of operations and services.

Orr, Pings, Pizer and Olson attempted to measure the effectiveness of academic medical libraries.[8] User satisfaction was chosen as the ultimate test of library effectiveness. The following criteria were selected to reflect user needs:

1. Obtaining documents
2. Locating citations
3. Receiving answers for specific needs
4. Having access to work space and facilities
5. Obtaining instruction and consultation

Librarians who simulated the user population were to obtain documents from a prepared list. The physical availability of the documents was scored on a Capability Index. The limitation inherent in this index is that the "score" represents a library's ability to deliver documents if its collection were not being used, i.e., whether a title is owned regardless of whether or not it is physically accessible to the patron.

Information services were tested by giving reference librarians 50 incomplete or incorrect citations to verify within a four hour period. Random alarm mechanisms (RAM) were used to sample staff activities. When an alarm bell rang, the staff member had to record what he was doing at that particular moment.

Another publication from this study described checklists of library policies which may be important to users.[9] These services were weighted to give a quantitative score. The checklist was used only with pre-test groups. No further reports of this study have been found in the literature since 1968.

Olson modified this checklist in his study of service policies in public, academic, special and school libraries in Indiana.[10] This study was the only one located which included a cross-section of types of libraries and also a large sample--over 1,000 libraries, half of which were school libraries.

There are serious questions about using this checklist to measure services. The librarians weight the importance of each service. Their opinions regarding these services may or may not coincide with those of their users. Also, this method relies solely on the veracity of the person checking the form. A service that is infrequently requested may be checked for maximum level service in terms of convenience to the patron. Yet, if the service were more frequently utilized it might be curtailed or deleted, e.g., free photo-copying.

The University of Lancaster studies have been primarily concerned with modeling the university library's ability to satisfy users' needs for materials in terms of circulation policies, availability of documents, duplication and time required to process in-coming materials, weeding, journal purchasing and inter-library loan. A "frustration survey" similar to the Capability Index was conducted among actual users.[11]

The Lancaster study is particularly interesting for two reasons. The researchers are librarians who have a good knowledge of statistics. Secondly, the models were actually implemented and library operations were changed as a result. This project demonstrates that research can have a practical and beneficial payoff.

The concern with optimum utilization of funds is reflected in four relatively recent studies: Hamburg,[12] Raffel and Shisko,[13] Durham University,[14] and Burkhalter.[15]

Morris Hamburg of the Wharton School of Finance developed "an allocation model" to apportion funding for the 49 outlets which comprise the Free Library of Philadelphia. The model is based on "document exposure time"--*i.e.*, the time spent reading both inside and outside the library. This model also includes such variables as population served, registered borrowers, circulation, in-library use, telephone queries, attendance, physical facilities, document resources, and educational level of the population. Reference service is considered only in terms of time and money.

All of these factors are related to costs. Hamburg concluded that "...it follows from the decision [of the City of Philadelphia] to invest in library services that each exposure hour produced by the Free Library has a monetary value of $0.72."[16] On a per capita basis this equals $0.46.[17] The methodology is based on the questionable assumption that people who return books can accurately remember how much time they spent reading each title. Hamburg claims this was 2.25 hours per title.[18] No attempt was made to find out whether circulated books were read completely, partially, or not at all. Yet, if a person read at the rate of 500 words per minute--a good rate--he could read 3,000 words per hour. If the average book contains 350 words per page that would mean the average number of pages read was 19.2.

Three library cost benefit studies are Raffel's and Shishko's at Massachusetts Institute of Technology, the Durham Computer Unit's study of Durham and Newcastle Universities in England, and Burkhalter's analysis of the University of Michigan Library. The M.I.T. researchers calculated costs for:

1. Open and closed access book storage
2. Book provision versus microform or xerox copies
3. Various types of reserve systems including cheap xerox, free xerox or microforms
4. Seating
5. Temporary cataloging
6. Rapid interlibrary loan
7. Weeding.

After current operational costs had been determined along with costs of changing the existing system, a questionnaire was sent to a random sample of faculty, graduate students and undergraduates. The three groups were asked to rank which services they would prefer to keep or to change within the limits of a $200,000 budget increase, a $100,000 increase, and no increase. Although the choices are not really applicable to public library operation, the findings illustrate the wide-ranging nature of user preferences. The undergraduates wanted centralized reserve, the graduate students wanted more books to check out while the faculty preferred departmental libraries. Obviously satisfying any group would be at the expense of the other two.

The title of the Durham study, "Projects for Evaluating the Benefits from University Libraries," promised more than the study delivered. Benefits are cast in terms of unit costs and the relationship between the cost of one service versus the cost of another. For example, the cost of adding one book is equivalent to obtaining 4.5 items on interlibrary loan or circulating 90 books on long-term loan. The premise is that once the library administrator has detailed cost and volume of activity data, he can better decide which services he wants to expand and which he wants to curtail to provide an optimum balance. He may or may not take needs or even demands into consideration. By this method the administrator evaluates the benefits offered by the library on the supposition that he is the best judge of "good" service for his institution.

Burkhalter's study is the best to date for analyzing library operations in terms of costs and alternate methods to reduce costs and/or improve efficiency. Burkhalter and a group of student engineers at the University of Michigan analyzed loan policies, inventory procedures, reshelving, periodical replacement and adequacy of seating at the University library. Costs of present methods were compared with likely alternates. This work is outstanding for its lucid presentation of mathematical computations and data-gathering procedures.

All of these studies relate to effectiveness in the broad sense in that they attempt to analyze some aspect of library service and devise ways to improve that service. We have outlined here only major recent works. Many other researchers have investigated a particular aspect of service such as library use, reference service and circulation. The amount of work that has been produced is illustrated by the 153 items contained in Slamecka's selective bibliography on library operations research.[19] Table 1 indicates the areas which the researchers cited here have analyzed and modeled in order to optimize performance and thus influence effectiveness. Table 2 shows the type of library, funding agency, and background of the researcher. The major strengths and weaknesses of the most important studies are outlined below.

Analysis of the studies completed to date prompts the following conclusions:

1. Most studies were done on individual libraries--primarily academic institutions which may or may not be similar to public libraries.

2. The research has not been cumulative. Some aspects of library operations like weeding, storage, duplication and unsatisfied demand have been done over and over again by different researchers. Yet, other critical areas have virtually been ignored--reference service, the library's impact on its community, optimum utilization of staff.

3. Most of these studies offer models which are essentially theoretical. The models are mathematically sound but are extremely difficult if not impossible to implement in a real situation.

4. The principal researchers involved in most of the mathematically-oriented studies have no library training or experience. Consequently some of the concepts presented and the approaches tried show a naivete about the complex nature of library activities.

5. Most of these reports describe the library as though the library staff did not exist. One wonders about the level of staff involvement in these studies. If staff involvement was minimal, it might be hypothesized that the studies had little impact on subsequent operations or service. Only the University of Lancaster has written on the actual implementation of the models prepared for that library.

6. Most of these studies, in order to be comprehended, require more knowledge of mathematics than the average librarian is likely to possess. Their impact on librarianship thus far appears to be minimal since no follow-up reports have appeared in the literature showing that these models have been adopted and/or adapted by other libraries.

The results of the literature search are clear. Few antecedent approaches exist which the public library can utilize fruitfully in developing innovative approaches to measuring the performance of the services it offers its public. Most earlier writings--pre-1960--stress the need for evaluation but no concrete explanations of how to proceed. The truth of this statement is verified by the fact that the profession is still searching for a "method." On the other hand, few of the newer approaches cited lend themselves to implementation and interpretation by the practicing librarian because of their reliance on highly sophisticated and complex methodologies.

The exceptions to the above observations are also limited in their usefulness to the public librarian who wants to utilize a fairly

TABLE 1

Author and Research Subject Matrix

Author	Document Demand	Circulation Policies	Duplicate Copies	Book Usage including Weeding & Storage Implications	Budget Allocation	Browsing	Seating	Tasks Performed by Patrons	Cataloging	Service Policies	Information Services	Reduction of Book Losses	Journal Purchases
Morse	X	X	X	X		X		X					X
Burkhalter		X	X		X		X					X	X
Lancaster University	X	X	X	X					X				
Durham University		X		X	X		X	X		X			X
Raffel & Shisko		X		X	X		X		X	X			
Hamburg	X	X		X	X		X						
Wessel (Thompson, Inc.)	X				X				X		X		
Pings, Pizer, Olson & Orr	X									X			
Olson										X	X		
Fussler & Simon				X									
Jain			X	X									
Trueswell	X		X	X									

TABLE 2 Relationship Between Type of Library, Researcher and Funding Agency — Author	Number of Libraries		Type of Library				Researcher		Source of Funds*		
	Multiple	Single	Academic	Special	Public	School	Non Librarian	Librarian	Outside	Library	Student Project
Morse		X	X				X		X		
Burkhalter		X	X				X			X	
Lancaster University		X	X					X		X	
Durham University	X		X				X				
Raffel & Shisko		X	X				X			X	
Hamburg	X		X		X		X		X		
Wessel (Thompson, Inc.)	X			X			X		X		
Pings, Pizer, Olson & Orr	X			X			X	X	X		
Olson	X		X	X	X	X	X		X		
Fussler & Simon	X		X				X				
Jain		X	X				X				X
Trueswell	X		X				X				

*In some cases, funding agency, if any, could not be determined.

broad-based program for evaluating and therefore measuring library services. For example, the unobtrusive method employed by Crowley and Childers is an ingenious approach for looking at the "quality performance" of one aspect of reference service: the accuracy of response to factual inquiries.[20] However, the unobtrusive approach could not be easily utilized by an administrator in assessing the answers given by his own reference staff. Not only would it be difficult to conceal that a test was being conducted, but it might have a debilitating effect on staff morale. Also, this method deals only with one aspect of the reference service program. This observation is not intended to deprecate in any way the usefulness of the method in certain selected instances, but rather, to suggest its limits for the broader objective suggested above.

In sum, there is little in the literature which is applicable to public libraries, or which can be understood and implemented by the practicing librarian. As a result, practicing librarians in attempting to assess the performance of the institutions have been forced to fall back on their major barometer of performance--library statistics.

NOTES

1/ Richard W. Trueswell, "A Quantitative Measure of User Circulation Requirements and Its Possible Effect on Stack Thinning and Multiple
Copy Determination," American Documentation, 16:20-5, 1965.

2/ Herman A. Fussler and J.L. Simon, Patterns In the Use of Books
in Large Research Libraries (University of Chicago Press, 1969).

3/ A. K. Jain, "Sampling and Short Period Usage in the Purdue
Library," College and Research Libraries, 27:211-8, 1966.

4/ Richard W. Trueswell, "Some Behavioral Patterns of Library
Users: the 80/20 Rule," Wilson Library Bulletin, 43:458-61, 1969.

5/ Philip M. Morse, Library Effectiveness (M.I.T. Press, 1968).

6/ John I. Thompson Company, Criteria for Evaluating the Effectiveness of Library Operations and Services. 1967-68 (ATLIS reports nos 10,
19, 21) 3v.

7/ C. J. Wessel, "Criteria for Evaluating Technical Library Effectiveness," ASLIB Proceedings, 20:455-81, 1968, p. 474.

8/ Richard H. Orr and others, "Development of Methodologic Tools
for Planning and Managing Library Services," Medical Library Association
Bulletin, 56:241-67, 380-403, 1968.

9/ Institute for the Advancement of Medical Communication, Checklist of Library Policies on Services to Individual Users (Philadelphia,
1968.

10/ Edwin E. Olson, Survey of User Policies in Indiana Libraries
and Information Centers. Indiana Library Studies. Report no. 10, 1970.

11/ Michael K. Buckland, System Analysis of a University Library
(University of Lancaster Library, 1970).

12/ Morris Hamburg and others, A Systems Analysis of the Library
and Information Science Statistical Data System (University of Pennsylvania, Wharton School of Finance and Commerce, 1970) 2v.

13/ Jeffery Raffel and Robert Shishko, Systematic Analysis of
University Libraries: An Application of Cost-Benefit Analysis to the
M.I.T. Libraries (M.I.T. Press, 1969).

14/ Durham University. Project for Evaluating the Benefits from
University Libraries: Final Report (Durham University Computer Unit,
1969).

15/ Barton R. Burkhalter, Case Studies in Systems Analysis in a
University Library (Scarecrow, 1968).

16/ Morris Hamburg, Leonard E. Ramist and Michael R. W. Bommer, "Library Objectives and Performance Measures and Their Use in Decision Making," _Library Quarterly_, 42:107-28, 1972.

17/ _Ibid._, p. 121.

18/ _Ibid._, p. 117.

19/ Vladimer Slamecka, "A Selective Bibliography on Library Operations Research," _Library Quarterly_, 42:152-158, 1972.

20/ Terrence Crowley and Thomas A. Childers, _Information Service in Public Libraries_ (Scarecrow, 1971).

3. Existing Library Statistics

Statistical information about public libraries is collected at three levels: local, state and federal. Individual libraries, for their own information, may collect data not required for their state reports, while state library reports may include information categories not used in the federal series.

The research team made no assumption regarding the adequacy of these statistics for purposes of measurement. Therefore, it was decided that the statistics collected at each level be identified and analyzed in detail to determine what data were available and the utility of these data for measuring library effectiveness. The following sections describe in detail these analyses of federal, state and local statistical reporting systems.

Federal Statistics

The United States Office of Education has published a series of selected statistical data for public libraries since 1944.[1] These statistics are used ostensibly for several purposes:[2]

1. To provide an internal statistical record for individual libraries and as an easy way to compare similar libraries.
2. To assist the federal government in decision-making.
3. To assist the public in evaluating the overall development of public libraries.

In practice, comparisons of libraries have been used extensively to show deficiencies in library service individually or collectively and consequently to justify a need for greater financial support. Implicit in this use, also, is that numerical quantities bear some relationship to actual performance or effectiveness. Larger quantities in almost all areas of service have commonly been presumed to mean better service. Although the validity of this relationship has been discussed widely in the literature for many years, the criticisms have generally focused on the need for so-called qualitative measures of performance rather than with substantive critiques and development of the quantitative measures themselves.

U.S.O.E. statistical reports for public libraries are totally descriptive. Numerical quantities are listed in each category with no attempt to analyze what these quantities mean or how they may be related to each other. In essence, a U.S.O.E. statistical report is a census of public libraries. Although modifications have been made in the data base in each publication, certain traditional categories have remained constant:

a. Population served

17

b. Size of collection
c. Total operating expenditure
d. Number of professional and clerical employees
e. Number of volumes added the previous year
f. Salary expenditures
g. Library material expenditures
h. Circulation[3]

Of these items, all except circulation and population are measures of __input__. Population is neither an input or an output. It is an uncontrolled variable. Circulation, as traditionally defined--number of items checked out of the building, reflects .the only attempt to determine output. For all of these items, accurate counting is essential if comparisons are to be useful or if totals are to be indicative of overall regional, state or national development. However, all parties concerned have not been able to agree on what constitutes these data categories or how they should be counted.

While U.S.O.E. has always recognized these problems, it has of practical necessity been required to publish the data essentially as submitted by the individual libraries while conceeding that much greater uniformity would be desirable. These same problems were encountered in this analysis and could only be handled by assuming accuracy in reporting; any deficiencies found in using the statistics as measures of effectiveness would therefore be accentuated if the data themselves were defective.

The purpose of the analysis of U.S.O.E. statistics was to determine their usefulness as measures of effectiveness. Therefore, we sought to answer two questions.

1. Could these data, as presently reported, be used as predictors?
    In other words, what are the relationships between books, total
    staff, money, professional staff, circulation and population and
    how do they influence each other? One might choose to explore
    other relationships using different, and perhaps more meaningful,
    variables. However, since this is a study of an existing statistical reporting system we could use only the information provided by the U.S.O.E. report.
2. What influence did size of library have on these statistics?
    Would relationships in the data differ according to the sizes of
    the units studied?

Since the Rockwoods' study in 1967 had determined that budget was the best indicator of library size,[4] a sample of 180 public libraries stratified by budget and geography was drawn from __Statistics of Public Libraries Serving Areas With at Least 25,000 Inhabitants. 1968.__[5]

Class of Library	Amount of Budget	Number in Sample
I. Small	$100,000-$ 249,999	71
II. Medium	$250,000-$ 749,999	61
III. Large	$750,000-$3,499,999	48
		180

Libraries with budgets less than $100,000 and more than $3,500,000 were omitted from this sample and all other phases of the project. These same size designations are used throughout the study. Insofar as possible, at least three libraries were chosen from each state--one from each budget class. For each of the sample libraries for the year 1968, the following data were taken from <u>Statistics</u> <u>of</u> <u>Public</u> <u>Libraries</u>.

1. Total operating expenditures
2. Population served
3. Library staff positions, excluding maintenance staff (in full-time equivalents)
4. Staff holding fifth-year degree in librarianship
5. Total salary expenditures, excluding maintenance salaries
6. Expenditures for library materials
7. Number of branches
8. Total book and serial holdings
9. Total book and serial volumes added during fiscal year
10. Total circulation (transactions of all materials lent for use outside the library during fiscal year

A computerized statistical test for determining predictive variables, stepwise multiple regression, was used. This test constructs a prediction equation one variable at a time by selecting the independent variable which is the best predictor of the dependent variable. The other variables are added step-by-step in order of importance until no other variable will contribute significantly to the equation.[6] The test was run separately for each of the three classes of libraries and for the entire sample. The findings showed that most variables are redundant in that they reflect different facets of the same measure--total operating expenditure. As a result, the correlations among these data tend to vary together in a consistent pattern. In other words, most of the data categories really "measure" the same thing--money. The only variable that have no monetary implications are circulation and population.

The final step in this analysis was to determine whether significant differences exist <u>between</u> the three library size categories.[7] To determine this it was necessary to have a common basis for comparing the size differences. The use of ratios provided such a base for each variable. Twenty-four ratios were computed for <u>each</u> individual library by dividing one variable by another.[8] The ratio categories used are given in the appendix. These ratios were ranked in each category for the entire sample and for the size-of-library subsamples. The ranked scores indicated that the data were not normally distributed. Also, the ranges and standard deviations were large for many categories.

Therefore, the median test was used. This approach is an application of chi-square to ordinal data to determine whether a significant difference exists in the scores of two or more samples. The common median is counted. The chi-square statistic is then calculated.[9] The chi-square statistic and the significance level for each ratio category are shown in the appendix.

Of the 24 ratios compared across the three classes, only 12 showed significant differences at the 0.05 level (See Table 3)   Nine of these 12 significant relationships dealt with some aspect of finance. Although large libraries spend almost $1.00 per capita more than the small librar- ies and 57¢ more than the medium libraries, there are no significant per capita differences in:

1. Volumes added
2. Service units
3. Amount spent for library materials
4. Circulation
5. Holdings
6. Library staff
7. M.L.S. staff

The logical question is where then does the money go? The answer is salaries. Large libraries on the average spend 62% of their budget for salaries, medium institutions 61% and small libraries 56%. The average annual salary in large libraries is $410 higher than in the medium librar- ies and $770 higher than in the small sized. Both the fraction of the budget spent for salaries and the amount of the median salary were signi- ficant at the 0.05 level.

One might logically hypothesize that the difference in salaries could be attributed to the presence of a higher proportion of profession- als (M.L.S. staff) in the larger libraries.[10] The hypothesis was dis- proven; the number of professionals as related to total staff was not significant among the three sizes of libraries. How then did the number of M.L.S. staff relate to other variables? In general, small and medium sized libraries had larger collections, added more volumes and circulated more materials per M.L.S. staff member. However, these statistics do not reflect specialized activities performed by professional staff in many libraries. In terms of total staff, only holdings per staff member proved significant--small libraries owned about 3,880 more volumes per employee than the large libraries while medium sized institutions owned 6,480 more than the large.

The relationship of holdings to circulation is significant in that large libraries had the lowest ratio of circulations per volume owned. Interestingly, there were no significant differences among the three groups between circulation and the number of volumes added or circulation and the amount of money spent for library materials.

Thus, using only the implied assumptions noted above, a statistical comparison of libraries of different sizes based on the data categories used in the U.S.O.E. report suggests that small libraries give a greater return per dollar spent, and that the economy of scale normally expected in larger institutions is not evident. Although this finding appears to contradict current economic theory, it may be a result of limitations in the data categories used in the U.S.O.E. report rather than in the fiscal management of the libraries studied. However, the preliminary results of the Wharton School Report (Morris Hamburg) suggests a similar conclusion by using a completely different statistical concept.[11]

Yet, such a conclusion would not be accepted by the most severe cri- tics of library service, and it is here that the librarians have justifiably

TABLE 3

Significance Levels for Median Test

	Total Expenditures	Salaries	Print Material Expenditures	Circulation	Holdings	Volumes Added	Library Staff	Population Served	Service Units
Total Expenditures		0.01	0.01	0.001		0.025			
Salaries			0.01						
Print Material Expenditures									
Circulation									
Holdings	0.025			0.05					
Volumes Added									
Library Staff	0.02	0.01		0.01					
MLS Staff					0.05				
Population Served	0.05								
Service Units									

Note: Blank columns indicate no significant relationships

fallen back on the demand for qualitative criteria which reflect the intangibles of a reference or outreach service. The lack of significant differences among so many items could mean, among other possibilities, that:

    a. Libraries of different sizes or stated functions are basically similar, or
    b. There are only a few true determinants of the form and quantity of library service.

Since this analysis is only a preliminary one using certain preset parameters, on can only say that U.S.O.E. statistics as now collected appear to have limited value

    a. in making valid comparisons
    b. as a basis for setting standards of development or performance
    c. to establish historical trend lines.

Why they have limited usefulness can only be hypothesized; perhaps these data categories were originally selected because they were easily counted. To the best of our knowledge, no one has ever made a conscientious effort to develop a theoretical or empirically based justification for the variables selected. This set of statistics however, does provide clues for formulating a more sophisticated system of statistics; and to this extent, plus the absence of other alternatives of measurement, they are an acceptable first generation tool. This project had the objective of developing a more sophisticated second generation model.

State Library Statistics

    All state library agencies were asked to provide copies of their latest public library statistical reports. Thirty-seven agencies responded. Analysis of these reports revealed the following: Forty-eight items, not all of which were statistics, were identified from the 37 state reports. Sixteen of these 48 appeared in 50% or more of the state reports. These 16 items, which are listed below, constitute the core of statistical reporting at the state level.

    1. Name, address and telephone number of library
    2. County
    3. Name of library director
    4. Name of library system, where applicable
    5. Population served
    6. Hours open per week or per day
    7. Total number of volumes added to collection
    8. Total number of volumes at year end
    9. Total circulation figures
    10. Income from local sources
    11. Income from state sources
    12. Income from other sources
    13. Total figure of all income sources
    14. Expenditure for salaries

15. Expenditure for library materials
16. Total figure for all expenditures

It can be seen that most statistics shown in state reports cover four basic facts about public libraries: book stock, circulation, income and expenditures. While useful as census data they remain, generalized reports which offer little direct evidence of effective service to the patron. Some state reports go beyond these sixteen basic items, giving: types of material held (New York), various sources of income (Pennsylvania), and unit costs estimates of certain services (Utah). The individual reports range freely, providing anything from the year of foundation (Colorado and Indiana) to numbers of reference transactions (California and South Carolina). A few states endeavor to put "life" into these statistics by reporting on the use made by the public of a service provided. California, Pennsylvania, and South Carolina, for example, provide figures on interlibrary loans. Iowa and Minnesota show the percentage of population unserved by libraries, although it is not clear if the figures relate to the lack of a library in a given area or, more important, that a percentage of the population does not avail itself of library service. Kansas breaks down total circulation figures in terms of loans to individuals/schools/hospitals/other institutions, which make these figures more meaningful. Indiana and Tennessee give details of bookmobile service showing the number of stops and kinds of patrons served. Some states provide a breakdown of audio-visual materials held, but neglect to provide circulation figures for these nonbook items. Finally, only nine states report on the numbers of professionals and nonprofessionals serving the patron. Like the federal report, the individual state statistics are descriptive. No attempt is made to relate the individual variables to each other or to assess the significance of the numbers as indicators of performance.

Public Library Questionnaire Survey

In September 1971, questionnaires were sent to a stratified sample of two hundred and fifty-four public libraries to determine the range of statistical data available with the idea that these data might be correlated with the measures developed in the study. Also we wanted input from practitioners as to what kinds of performance measures they thought would be most useful. The sample, drawn from the American Library Directory, 1971, [12] was stratified by size and geographic area. While all libraries used in the U.S.O.E. statistics analysis were included, the American Library Directory was used for selecting this sample for the following reasons:

1. All libraries serving populations under 25,000 inhabitants are excluded from the federal report regardless of their budget size.
2. No libraries in the state of Georgia were included in the 1968 report.
3. American Library Directory gave more current budget figures.

Since there is considerable variation in the size of libraries, this variable had to be taken into consideration in any attempt to measure

effectiveness. Libraries with greater resources might be able to offer
a broader range of programs, specialized services and the like; elements
that may be lacking in other libraries due to their more limited resources.
In such a case, comparison would be misleading. Since budget was used
to determine size in other phases of this study it was also used to
categorize the libraries in this sample. The same budget categories were
used throughout.

Small Libraries	$100,000 - $ 249,999
Medium Libraries	$250,000 - $ 749,999
Large Libraries	$750,000 - $3,499,999

There was also an attempt to obtain an equitable geographical distribution within the sample.

The one hundred and twenty-four respondents to this questionnaire
answered eighty-five questions regarding the ease or difficulty that
their library would have in providing different types of information for
the last five years. Each library was asked to respond in the following
way to each of the items:

E--Easy to Provide

I have the exact figure(s) requested
or a very similar breakdown in my
files and records.

D--Difficult to Provide

I do not have the exact figure(s) on
hand, but my files or records contain
the information which would allow me
to compute the requested figure(s).

I--Impossible to Provide

I have neither the exact figure(s) on
hand nor the files or records to compute the necessary figure(s). I would
be required to set up a new record-
keeping system or do a special study
in order to provide the information.

C--Detailed Records are not
     Retained

The information is currently collected
but a record for past years is not
retained.

N--Not Applicable

On the basis of the responses to these questions, an analysis of the
availability of different types of information was made. The following
list provides a breakdown on the relative availability of the eighty-five
items for all libraries responding and by budget category.

TABLE 4

Availability of Library Statistics--1965-1970

Information Available For:	Number & Percent of Libraries in Sample			
	Total (124)	Large (34)	Medium (43)	Small (47)
Total square feet in building	98%	100%	98%	98%
Budgeted amount--equipment/supplies	98	97	100	96
Total volumes in collection	98	97	98	100
Total volumes added yearly	98	97	98	98
Total volumes withdrawn	98	94	100	98
Annual per capita expenditure	97	97	98	96
Total population in service area	96	100	95	94
Budgeted amount--professional salaries	94	94	98	89
Budgeted amount--nonprofessional salaries	94	94	98	89
Total square feet of stack area	94	94	93	94
Total square feet of reading room	94	91	95	96
Budgeted amount--building maintenance	93	94	95	89
Budgeted amount--print resources	90	94	91	87
Total--phonograph records	89	94	88	85
Budgeted amount--nonprint resources	87	94	86	83
Total items circulated yearly	87	91	86	85
Total ILL items borrowed annually	86	91	86	83
Total ILL items loaned annually	82	85	91	72
Total microforms in collection	82	82	86	79
Total periodical titles	82	82	74	89
Total registered borrowers	81	71	81	87
Total other A-V materials	79	79	65	58
Hours of staff time on building maintenance	78	79	81	75
Total juvenile fiction volumes	78	74	81	79
Hours of staff time on technical services	77	79	81	72
Hours of staff time on circulation	77	79	79	72
Hours of staff time on administration	76	76	81	70
Hours of staff time on reference	73	74	77	70
Total juvenile nonfiction volumes	73	68	75	77
Total films in collection	71	88	70	60
Total juvenile registered borrowers	71	65	68	79
Annual per-registered-borrower expenditure	71	59	74	77
Total adult registered borrowers	70	62	68	79

TABLE 4 (Continued)

Availability of Library Statistics--1965-1970

Information Available For:	Number & Percent of Libraries in Sample			
	Total (124)	Large (34)	Medium (43)	Small (47)
Total adult/young adult non-fiction volumes	69%	62%	77%	68%
Total adult/young adult fiction volumes	69	59	79	66
Total reference volumes	68	68	67	68
Percent staff time spent at reference desk	68	59	74	68
Total circulation--audio visual materials	66	82	65	55
Hours staff time on organization and maintenance of collection	65	65	65	64
Hours staff time on public relations	64	71	58	64
Total periodical volumes	61	62	65	58
Percent time spent selecting books	57	41	60	64
Total titles added yearly	56	85	61	32
Total filmstrips in collection	53	56	58	47
Total volumes lost yearly	50	50	58	43
Total circulation of adult fiction	50	44	47	57
Total circulation adult nonfiction	50	44	47	57
Number of ILL requests not satisfied	49	47	49	51
Total circulation--juvenile fiction	48	44	42	55
Budgeted amount--technical services	46	56	51	34
Total circulation--juvenile nonfiction	46	41	42	53
Budgeted amount--administration	44	53	51	30
Amount received to provide system services	41	50	49	28
Budgeted amount--circulation	40	53	47	26
Amount spent for system services	39	35	49	32
Total circulation--periodicals	38	29	32	49
Total titles withdrawn yearly	36	29	49	28
Budgeted amount--reference services	35	44	40	23
Hours of staff time on system activities	34	44	35	21
Total titles in collection	34	38	42	23
Number requests sent via tele-transmission	33	47	35	21
Budgeted amount--other reader services	33	44	37	21

TABLE 4 (Continued)

Availability of Library Statistics--1965-1970

Information Available For:	Number & Percent of Libraries in Sample			
	Total (124)	Large (34)	Medium (43)	Small (47)
Number requests received via teletransmission	32%	47%	33%	21%
Number reference questions referred elsewhere	32	27	33	36
Total reference titles	32	21	37	36
Total government documents	31	50	33	17
Total adult/young adult fiction titles	31	32	42	21
Total adult/young adult nonfiction titles	31	32	40	23
Total juvenile fiction titles	31	24	47	23
Total juvenile nonfiction titles	29	21	42	23
Number reference requests answered for others	28	27	28	30
Number items lent to universal borrowers	24	18	30	23
Number patrons entering building daily	23	35	21	15
Budgeted amount--(unspecified) other	23	21	26	23
Total titles lost yearly	23	18	35	17
Number reference questions referred but not answered	22	12	21	30
Budgeted amount--system membership	17	12	26	13
Number requests received via WATS line	10	9	12	9
Number requests sent via WATS line	8	3	12	9
Budgeted amount--other (unspecified) area	7	9	7	6
Total circulation government documents	6	18	2	2
Number requests sent via tie lines	5	0	9	4
Number requests received via lease lines	4	0	9	2
Number requests sent via lease lines	4	0	7	4
Number requests received via tie lines	3	0	7	2

The Usefulness of Public Library Statistics

Librarians in the national questionnaire were asked what measures of quality, which could be statistically determined, they would like to have available for use in evaluating their services. As one might expect, a variety of responses were reported. However, the responses, once categorized, revealed a clear desire for more information directly related to the user.

Basically, the suggestions centered around user satisfaction and user activity. Thus, for example, one librarian suggested the following:

> A record of individual patron satisfaction and dissatisfaction for every service transaction between him and the library. A rating scale for numbers of people in the service area reached in some way by library service compared to other agency ratings. (This comparison could also be made with other libraries using the same criteria.)

Another librarian noted: "Judgment of each person who uses the library during the year as to how well he was served by it and a report from him on areas where he was not served well." Another said: "Mainly, some measure of patrons' reaction or a statement as to their satisfaction with the library's response or service."

Intuitively, these librarians were saying that the data currently collected is not people or user-oriented. The decision to simulate the user through the methodology of probability statistics was reinforced by these responses. The data collection approach, as illustrated in the Instructional Manual for the Collection of Selected Public Library Information,[13] sharply demonstrates the efforts of the research team to fill the user-oriented information gap.

The same librarians were asked to indicate which statistics could be reported which would accurately reflect their library's effectiveness. Again, the responses centered around the user, as contrasted to "things". The following observations made by these librarians illustrate this point:

> "Written or verbal testimonies of people--numbers do not show effectiveness."
> "None, unless we place a counter on the door to count the number of patrons each day."
> "Number of people who went away dissatisfied (or unsatisfied)."
> "Number of people using the library--not just circulation--especially in special collections. Requests not filled. What percentage of patrons are not finding what they want."
> "Gallup-type polling of representative samples of the public at different times might do it. Certainly circulation figures and borrowers registered don't."

Of course, some librarians responded by noting that they "doubt that such statistics exist" and "you tell me."

These librarians were also asked to comment on the use of statistics to measure effectiveness. From the responses received, it is not difficult to see how doubtful they are that one can measure effectiveness statistically. Representative comments were:

> "Statistics do not evaluate quality of service or degree of
> satisfaction of community and/or patron needs. I know no way
> this can be measured statistically."
>
> "Statistics as kept do not describe the quality/nature of individual service—only the volume of it. I don't think statistics—
> numbers—or non-verbal written data can describe the humanistic
> situation in the subjective atmosphere in which it takes place."
>
> "Statistics can be misleading and none can give a complete picture of library service. I abhor the time involved in too many
> 'statistical reports' and do wish a uniform system could be
> devised that would satisfy all types of libraries—don't you."
>
> "Statistics do not and I don't believe could ever include the
> human factor in giving service which I believe to be the key.
> I do not think that it is possible to reflect statistically the
> effectiveness of a devoted reference librarian or a children's
> librarian unless a person was asked to fill out a brief questionnaire each time he used the library. Business men often do not
> need help and know how to use the services and directories. It
> would be difficult to measure the library's effectiveness to
> this extent without invading privacy."

These comments indicate the kinds of reservation which public librarians have about the statistical measurement of effectiveness. However, when all of their responses are viewed together, it is also clear that public librarians need and want better and more appropriate ways of "measuring" the services they offer through some kind of user-orientation rather than the current "thing-oriented" approach. The aims of this study attempted to meet this clearly expressed need.

NOTES

1/ National Center for Education Statistics, <u>Statistics of Public Libraries Serving Areas with at Least 25,000 Inhabitants</u>. <u>1968</u>. (G.P.O., 1970), p. iii. Hereafter referred to as NCES, <u>Statistics of Public Libraries</u>.

2/ Carol A. Salverson, "Relevance of Statistics to Library Evaluation," <u>College and Research Libraries</u>, 30:352-61, 1969.

3/ NCES, <u>Statistics of Public Libraries</u>.

4/ Ruth Rockwood and Charles Rockwood, <u>Quantitative Guides to Public Library Operations</u>. Illinois University. Graduate School of Library Science. Occasional paper. 1967.

5/ NCES, <u>Statistics of Public Libraries</u>.

6/ Norman Nie, Dale H. Brent and C. Hadlai Hull, <u>SPSS: Statistical Package for the Social Sciences</u> (McGraw-Hill, 1970), pp. 180-1.

7/ The term "significant difference" is used in a statistical sense--not attributable to chance.

8/ Since data on ten variables were available, there were 55 possible ratio categories. However, 21 of these ratios were meaningless.

9/ For a fuller explanation of this test see: John T. Roscoe, <u>Fundamental Research Statistics for the Behavioral Sciences</u> (Holt, Reinhart and Winston, 1969), pp. 201-2.

10/ It was previously stated that M.L.S. staff <u>per capita</u> was not significantly different among the three groups.

11/ Morris Hamburg, (Director), Richard C. Clelland, Michael R.W. Bommer, Leonard E. Rarmist, Donald M. Whitfield, <u>Library Planning and Decision-Making Systems</u>. U.S. Department of Health, Education, and Welfare, Bureau of Libraries and Education Technology, Final Report, December 1972.

12/ R.R. Bowker, Inc., <u>American Library Directory</u>, 1971 (Bowker, 1971).

13/ Rutgers University. Graduate School of Library Service. Bureau of Library and Information Science Research. <u>Instruction Manual for the Collection of Selected Public Library Information</u> (Bureau of Library and Information Science Research, n.d.)

4. Methodology

The primary purpose of this study was to develop meaningful indicators of performance which could be used by library administrators
to assess the effectiveness of their operations. Therefore, all measurement criteria had to conform to the following constraints:

1. Data required for the measurement tests must be collectable
    at the local level
2. The data collection must be amenable to the use of sam-
    pling techniques
3. The measurement criteria must differentiate between
    libraries
4. The measurement criteria should be capable of supplement-
    ing or replacing existing statistical reporting systems
5. The measurement tests, while objectively based, should
    be constructed in a manner suitable for interpretation by
    practicing librarians
6. The data collected should provide administrators with a
    tool for internal management and decision making.

In viewing existing public library services, it is both necessary
and useful to develop a basic framework within which to look at these
services. In the early stages of this project we attempted to list all
the things (items, services, conveniences) different users might want
or expect from a public library. The list grew to voluminous proportions.
While we would liked to have included most or even all of these items
it became apparent that the data gathering would require such a monumen-
tal effort on the part of the staffs of the participating libraries that
we were forced to reduce the list to more modest proportions.
Therefore, we confined the measurement criteria to basic services
traditionally and universally provided by public libraries:

1. Making materials available to users
2. Providing facilities to users
3. Making staff available to users

By analyzing existing library services through these three broad
areas, we can stress accomplishments in terms of these services. His-
torically we have been forced to look at "things" or inputs, such as
total number of books, and then make the substantial jump as to how these
"things" translate into services.
Further, by focusing on how well these services are performed, we
can better understand the variety of public libraries and the ways in

which overall resources, physical facilities, user populations, and so forth, integrate. With this approach, we should expect to see differences between smaller and larger public library operations, which current statistical reporting systems do not show.

Ideally, we would like to have included all units in the systems of the sample libraries--whether that system was main library and branches or regional system. This was impossible because of limited staff and limited funds. Therefore, although some elements include branches and/or regional systems, where applicable, these are minimal. The focus of the study is on the main library as an independent unit.

Many concepts presented here are not "new" to those who are familiar with the research literature. However, we believe this is the first attempt to integrate a number of these elements to produce a profile of effectiveness for public libraries. This profile is potentially a valuable tool for management decision-making.

Pretest, Pilot Libraries and Instructional Manual

The methodology for the study was developed and pretested in four pilot libraries during Phase II. Following innumerable staff sessions, dialogue with library educators and practicing librarians, plus a preliminary analysis of the results of the literature search, the decision was made to select three medium-sized public libraries of "like character"--similar in terms of budget, size of collection, number of branches, number of employees, and so forth. The results of the pilot would provide a basis on which to make initial judgments regarding the forms used to collect the data and the sufficiency of the data itself.

The project staff proceeded to develop the method and reporting forms and then do the actual collection of the data in the pilot libraries. In this way the research team could gather first-hand knowledge about the adequacy of the forms, identify problems which the data gathering approach might present to local librarians, and determine the time required to collect the information. One of the pilot libraries was generous enough to provide a member of its staff who worked on the research team on a part-time basis. Consequently, we were able to have an effective link for feedback on the methodology as an integral part of the research operation.

With the completion of the data gathering in the three pilot libraries, an instructional manual was drafted.[1] This manual outlined step-by-step procedures for the data collection and included copies of the reporting forms to be used by the participating libraries. We then decided to select one more library to test the manual, that is, to see if a local library could collect the information within the limits established. It was assumed that a key element in any data collection is the existence of sufficient staff. Consequently, staff size might very well be a problem with the "small" public library. As a result, the director of a small library was asked to participate in the study. A special one day workshop on data collection procedures, following the instructions provided in the manual, was conducted for this director by the research team. The director then took the manual and gathered the data with a minimum of difficulty in her own library.

The major goals of the pretest, then, were to see: (1) if data could be collected on each criterion or item, (2) if a library could collect the data on its own with minimum supervision, and (3) if each item was discriminatory—did it show individuality or, in combination with other items, differences in the four libraries which professionally trained librarians could observe in a gross sense or surmise from interviewing employees? It was assumed that most significant criteria or items had an outward manifestation in the form of some kind of quantifiable action or statistics. This assumption was made for research purposes and does not mean that the project personnel believe that all aspects of library programs can be or should be translated into statistics.

The data collected in the four pilot libraries was refined and analyzed before any major decisions were made regarding Phase III. Naturally, the critical factor was whether or not the measurement indicators selected did, in fact, discriminate among the services offered by different libraries. The results of the pilot data analysis satisfied the project personnel that the Phase III undertaking would be viable.

Phase III - National Sample, Workshops and Library Profiles

We then proceeded to select 20 libraries for Phase III. The selection was influenced by a number of factors. The most important were: (1) geographical spread, (2) budget distribution to fall within our small, medium and large size categories, and (3) a commitment to the overall objectives of the project by the library director. Data collection was planned to cover a two-week period. Roughly fifty-five hours of time was required to collect the desired information during week one of the study. A commitment of three full days was required in week two. In addition, each participating library was asked to appoint a project coordinator to supervise the data collection and forward the results to the Research Bureau at Rutgers. In order to approximate "normal" conditions, the libraries participating in the study were asked to give no prior publicity to the project.

Three regional training workshops were conducted for the project coordinators appointed by the libraries participating in Phase III. The first workshop was given in New Brunswick, New Jersey; the second in Atlanta, Georgia; and the third in San Francisco, California. The workshop sessions stressed the methodology of the data collection process. Generally, the project coordinators had no problems in comprehending the instructions.

They returned to their libraries and supervised the gathering and recording of the data on the standardized forms provided by the Rutgers Research Bureau. However, most of the data was collected by clerks and/ or volunteers. All data was forwarded to Rutgers for analysis.

Each of the participating libraries has received a profile of its scores on the measurement criteria which show how each score relates to those of other libraries of similar size. An example of one of the profiles is presented and discussed on pages 47-57.

Measurement Criteria

In developing the measurement criteria, we tried to keep the user in focus at all times. Where it was feasible to use real users, we did. In other instances, the libraries' staffs simulated users. The criteria are based on three services common to all public libraries and reflect those areas basic to user needs: collection, facilities, and staff assistance.

Materials Availability. With few exceptions public libraries have not yet entered the world of "non-print." Well over 95 percent of public library material is print.[2] Consequently, materials availability is measured in terms of the book and periodical collections made available to the user.

A library is similar to a warehouse in that a large volume of stock is in continual flux. Two factors influence the turnover of this inventory: supply of available materials and demand for that supply. Supply is affected by the number of new materials added to the collection, by the number of items withdrawn or lost and by demand for those items already in stock. Demand is determined by such intangible factors as the nature of the community and its myriad needs for library materials and the previous success users have experienced in obtaining items from the library. Like a warehouse, a library receives requests or "orders" for material in the following categories:

1. Items not owned
2. Items owned but presently unavailable
3. Items owned and available.

From these three conditional states it is possible to compute both the probability that a library will own a title and the probability of the title being available on the shelf and thus estimate users' "success rates" in obtaining materials from a library or from a group of libraries.

The two methods employed in assessing collection availability were sampling and simulation. The research team prepared the sampling methodology. The library staff acted as "users" in attempting to locate the materials in the following categories:

1. Recently published books
2. Periodicals
3. Titles already in the library's collection.

Recently Published Books. Previous research has established that recent books are requested and circulated more frequently than other titles in the collection.[3] Since this is so, this type of material should be considered separately from the rest of the collection.

In estimating the chances a user has in obtaining recently published books, two probability factors must be established:

1. The probability that the library owns the book, and
2. The probability that the title will be on the shelf.

By probability we mean the number of successful outcomes in 100 occurrences. Thus, a probability of 0.37 means that for every 100 attempts to obtain an item, 37 will be successful.

To determine these probabilities a sequential sample of 500 titles was drawn from American Book Publishing Record for the years 1966-1970. (Hereafter, this will be referred to as the BPR sample.) These sample titles are not considered as recommended in any sense. They are simply a group of titles published within a five-year period.

The public catalog was used to determine how many of these 500 were in the collection of the main library and its branches. From this figure it was possible to compute the "Probability of Ownership," (O). For example, if a library owned 200 of the books, its Pr(O) = 0.40, i.e. (200/500). Since some of these titles were new editions or reprints, the libraries were given credit for having previous editions and original copies.

The shelves were searched to ascertain how many of the owned titles were physically available. This number is then used to calculate the "Availability of Books Owned Probability" (B). If 75 of the 200 owned books were on the shelves, Pr(B) = 0.375, i.e. (75/200). Using these two probability figures, the "Probability of Availability" (A) can be determined. Pr(A) estimates a user's chances of actually obtaining any title listed in BPR for the five-year period. Pr(O) X Pr(B) = Pr(A), i.e. (0.40 X 0.375 = 0.15). Thus, a user has 15 chances in a hundred of getting a recently published book in this example.

In the libraries studied, the "Probability of Ownership" ranges from slightly less than eight chances in one hundred to nearly 58. For those BPR titles which are owned the chances of finding one on the shelves ranges from 55 to 81 percent. The user's chances are, on the average, highest in the medium-sized library where seven out of ten books are on the shelves. The "Probability of Availability" varies from less than one out of ten chances to slightly less than six in ten. The averages were 27 percent for large libraries, 18 percent for medium libraries and 8 percent for small libraries. A detailed breakdown of the figures mentioned here and in succeeding sections can be found in Chapter 5. This BPR sample also provides information on the availability status of adult and juvenile titles and the subject distribution of these titles according to Dewey Classification.

Periodicals. Eighty citations to periodical articles covering the years 1966-1970 were drawn from the following common indexes: Social Science and Humanities Index, Business Periodicals Index, Biological and Agricultural Index, Applied Science and Technology Index, Education Index, Art Index, Public Affairs Information Service and Readers' Guide.

Each library was to ascertain if it owned the journal cited whether in print or microfilm. The number owned was used to calculate the "Probability of Ownership," Pr(O) = 0.50, i.e. (40/80). Then, checks were made to verify if the specific article cited was available--the issue was in the library and the article had not been ripped out. The number of articles actually available was used to compute the "Availability of Articles Owned" (C). If 35 were available, Pr(C) = 0.875, i.e. (35/40). The "Probability of Availability" was determined by Pr(O) X Pr(C) = Pr(A), i.e. (0.50 X 0.875 = 0.44).

The probability of a public library's owning any particular periodical ranges greatly both within the same sized libraries as well as between various sized libraries. The percentage range in large public libraries is from 18 to 95; in medium-sized libraries the range is from 26 to 45; and in the small, it runs from 10 to 26. However, if the library owns the periodical, the user has about nine chances out of ten of finding the particular article. However, the "Probability of Availability" varies from 9 percent to 95 percent overall. The average Pr(A) for the different sizes of libraries are 0.45 for large, 0.31 for medium, and 0.18 for small.

Titles in the Library's Collection. Five hundred titles were drawn from each library's shelflist. The sequential sampling procedure insured that these titles represented a cross-section of that library's collection. Titles held only in branches were also included. The shelf availability of each book was verified to determine a user's probability in obtaining titles already owned by the library.

The number of titles actually available divided by 500 gives the "Shelf Availability Probability" (S) for that library. Pr(S) = 0.60, i.e. (300/500).

On the whole, the user can expect fairly good success, from 0.58 to 0.89 probability. One has the best chance of locating a book in the medium-sized library, slightly more than eight chances in ten. In general, children's books are less available than those for adults.

This title availability sample also provides data on the age of the collection, the ratio of adult to juvenile books and the proportion of titles in the various Dewey classes.

Facilities' Use

Effective library service requires some knowledge of the people who come to the library, at what hours of the day, for how long a time, and the use these people make of the library's collection, facilities and services. Information was collected on the following:

1. Building usage
2. Circulation
3. Furnishings and equipment use

These data were collected simultaneously during three days of the same week. Each library selected its own days to represent light, medium and heavy use of the building.

Building Usage. A clerk, page or volunteer was stationed at each entrance for the entire time the library was open on the three chosen days. That person marked the time of arrival of each patron on a small ticket. The ticket was given to the patron to be filled out and returned to the monitor when the patron left the building. The monitor then recorded the departure time. The tickets provided the following information about the library's clientele:

1. Description of users
2. User satisfaction
3. Time spent in the building.

Information requested on the ticket was deliberately held to a minimum
to encourage patron response. The response level was very high, about
98 percent.

Description of Users. Users, in this case, were defined as persons entering the library. Staff members and those on business calls
such as typewriter repairmen, and mailmen were excluded. The description categories were:

1. Sex
2. Student-Nonstudent
3. Grade Level of Students
4. Occupation of Nonstudents

As one might expect, more women than men used the small public
library, about 55 percent to 45 percent. However, contrary to many
views, more men than women used the large public library, about 60 percent to 40 percent. We did not find more than 60 percent of any one sex
using the library.

A breakdown of student users by grade level reveals some important
distinctions. In toto, more students (52 percent) use small public
libraries than large ones, (36 percent). Of the students using the
large public library, 34 percent are college level. On the other hand,
college students constitute only 13 percent of all student use in the
small public library. More high school students use medium and large
institutions. But, the lower the grade level the more likely it is that
the student will use the smaller library. For example, elementary
school students represent only 9 percent of the student use in large
public libraries, 25 percent in medium-sized, and 31 percent in small
libraries. High school students constitute the heaviest class of student patrons, 35 percent in the large library, 30 percent in the medium,
and 28 percent in the small.

Professional and white collar workers account for 57 percent of all
non-student use in large public libraries. The proportion of use by
these two groups drops to 36 percent in the smaller library.

The reverse is true for housewives. From an average of 32 percent
in the small public library their representation drops to 8 percent in
the larger library.

Use of the public library by blue collar workers is relatively even,
regardless of the size of the library, ranging between 10 and 13 percent.
The same is true for the retired, averaging about 9 percent. Unemployed
users range from about 1 percent in the small library to about 3 percent
in the large.

User Satisfaction. Users assessed their general satisfaction based
on their most recent experience in the library. Users of small libraries in this study tend to be the most satisfied, although the range by
size of library is not great--67 percent (large) to 72 percent (small).
When those users who checked "partially satisfied" are included with
the "satisfied," the range is 87 percent (large), 86 percent (medium),
and 89 percent (small). Roughly, only 7 percent of the users expressed
dissatisfaction.

Time Spent in the Building. This information was obtained from the tickets. Time spent has proven to be an excellent discriminator between libraries because it affects use of materials within the building, use of seats and equipment, and use and deployment of staff. The time data from the pilot libraries confirmed our on-the-scene impressions. One library could be characterized as a quick-lunch counter. Many people entered but left within a fifteen minute period. Another pilot library was exactly the opposite. Fewer people came, but those who did spent an hour on the average. As a result, the staff was asked many more reference questions. Use of materials in the building was extremely high although few people checked anything out for home use.

Based on the sample in this study, peak-use hours vary by size of library. Small libraries have heaviest use from late afternoon to evening. Mid-to-late-afternoon is peak time in medium-sized libraries and from noon to five in the large. These findings have obvious implications for staffing patterns. The time patrons spend in the building can be calculated to measure overall performance and also can be related to user characteristics. We can estimate effective user hours for our three-day sampling period in the following way:

1. H = number of hours open during the three days, (36)
2. W = sum of hours spent by users in the library during the same three days, (412).

Therefore, effective user hours, $EH = W/H = 11.44$, i.e. (412/36). This figure represents 11.4 hours of user time for each hour that the library was open.

We can calculate effective user hours for each user group in the same manner by simply adding the hours spent by each group and each sub-group.

For example, let:

W_1 = hours spent by all students (600)
W_{1a} = hours spent by elementary school students (120)
W_{1b} = hours spent by high school students (300)
W_{1c} = hours spent by college students (180)

Thus, effective user hours of college students is $EH = W_{1c}/H = 5$, i.e. (180/36).

Circulation. Traditionally reported circulation figures represent only those items removed from the library. However, certain kinds of materials--newspapers, microfilms, tapes, vertical file items and periodicals--are restricted to use in the building by most libraries.

Because use of these types of material is omitted from most, if not all, presently collected circulation statistics, we decided to monitor both "inside" and "outside" circulation concurrently with monitoring use of the building.

In-Library Circulation. This is an estimate based on an hourly count of the types of items being used by patrons plus all materials which are left on tables. This measure gives an estimate of both the form and frequency of materials being used as well as the proportion of total in-library circulation represented by each type. Separate records were kept for adult and juvenile items.

For libraries in this study, materials used in the building account-ed for at least 25 percent of all items circulated. In some of the li-braries, in-library circulations nearly equaled all outside circulation. Differences in the use of certain materials varied according to the size of the library--heavy use of encyclopedias in small libraries with high use of newspapers and microfilm in the larger institutions.

Outside Library Circulation. These data were collected by the staff at each circulation desk in the library. Information was tabulated not only on the number of items circulated but also on the number of per-sons checking out materials. From these figures we can calculate the percentage of persons entering the library who actually borrowed mater-ials and the average number of items circulated per borrower. A higher percentage of users checked out books in medium-sized libraries than in either larger or smaller ones. However, the number of items borrowed per person averages approximately three, ragardless of library size. A most important finding is that borrowers, on the average, range from one-third to less than one-half of all persons who enter the building. Obviously, the public library which still attempts to "evaluate" its performance solely on circulation figures is shortchanging itself!

To give a more realistic picture of library use, we need a method to take in-library circulations into account. Ideally, we could have patrons record on the tickets their separate totals for in and outside circulation. However, making the ticket longer would undoubtedly in-crease resistance to answering and might raise questions concerning pa-tron privacy. Therefore we will _estimate_ a library's actual circulation per user.

Let: EC = effective circulations per user
U = all persons entering building (1500)
U_B = all persons checking out material for use outside the library (500)
C_I = total inside circulation (760)
C_O = total outside circulation (1500)

$$EC = (C_O /U_B) + (C_I/U) = 3.5, \text{ i.e. } (1500/500) + (760/1500) = 3.5)$$

Facilities Usage. During the first week of the study, data were collected on the type and number of facilities available for patron use. These included number of seats, typewriters, micro-readers, photocopiers, audio and video equipment and meeting rooms. During the three-day moni-toring period, hourly checks were made to determine what equipment was being used at what hours of the day. We found that only two types of facilities and equipment received any substantial use. These were seats and meeting rooms. The only equipment having any appreciable use were photocopiers, microfilm readers and record players. These findings are similar for all size-of-library categories.

We can use these figures on number and use of facilities and equip-ment to determine effective equipment use (EQ).

Let: H = total number of hourly counts equipment use is recorded
        (36)
      B = sum of all equipment (50)
B can be divided into separate equipment categories such as:
      B_1 = seats
      B_2 = record players
      B_3 = microfilm readers
U_J = sum of recorded users of equipment (150)
      U_{J_i} = users of specific equipment such as seats, microfilm
            readers, record players, etc.

Thus, $EQ = U_J/(HB) = 0.08$, i.e. $(150/1800 = 0.08)$
EQ can never exceed 1 which is maximum use at all times. To calculate
effective use of any specific type of equipment: $EQ = U_{J_i}/(HB_i)$.

<u>Patterns of Reference Usage</u>. Public service staff were asked to
record all interactions with patrons to provide the following information.

1. Time question posed.
2. Whether the questioner was an adult, a student, or another
    library.
3. Whether the question was posed in person, by phone or by mail.
4. Whether the question was answered or not.
5. Whether the question was source-related or directional. That
    is: was library material required to provide the answer?
6. If source-related, what source or sources were used?

Admittedly, these data do not disclose how well the reference questions
were answered, but they do indicate gross activity and its implications
for staffing patterns.
    Two significant pieces of information were discovered from this
measure.

1. Source-related questions, those requiring use of library
    materials, accounted for only one-third to less than one-half
    of all questions asked, regardless of the size of the library.
2. Although many of the libraries in this study were headquarters
    for intra-city branches or regional systems, question referral
    from and to other libraries was virtually non-existent.

Most reference activity occurs between 9 a.m. and 6 p.m. regardless
of the size of the library. The number of transactions per hour ranged
from 12 to 500. The average was about 60 per hour for the majority of
the libraries studied, but four large libraries averaged close to 200
questions per hour.
    In public libraries of every size, adults asked the most questions,
averaging 52 percent in small and medium-sized libraries to 76 percent
in the large. Telephone questions accounted for nearly half of all questions asked in large libraries, but for less than 20 percent in the other
size-of-library categories.
    <u>Public Service Personnel</u>. A questionnaire was filled out by all

personnel who normally answered questions from patrons. Data were gathered regarding their age, sex, length of employment at the library, years of library experience, education, number of hours per week at public service desks and hourly scheduling patterns. These last two items allow us to make several calculations which describe the relationships between public service staff and users. These can be computed on any time basis desired. The following examples refer to the three-day study period.

Let: U = users (4559)
U_H = all reference patrons in building (2515)
U_S = patrons in the building asking source-related questions (515)
Q = all questions, including phone and mail (3215)
S = source-related questions (953)
P = public service staff hours (279)
H = the number of hours the library is open (36)

1. The ratio of total users to reference patrons in the building: U/U_H = 1.8, i.e. 4559/2515.
2. The ratio of all users to patrons asking source related questions: U/U_S = 8.9, i.e. 4559/515.
3. The ratio of persons in the building to public service staff hours: U/P = 16.3, i.e. 4559/279.
4. The number of questions answered per hour of staff time: Q/P = 11.5, i.e. 3215/279.
5. The number of source related questions per hour of staff time: S/P = 3.4, i.e. 953/279.

Library Programs

We have heard over and over again during the past few years that the quality of a library is reflected in programs which cannot be quantifiably measured. We agree that certain aspects of library programming do not lend themselves easily to measurement, for example the knowledge or enjoyment which the individual participants gained by their attendance. However, we feel that certain things can be examined:

1. The number of programs held.
2. The variety of programming.
3. The different groups within the community who have been served by these programs.

The participating libraries were asked to provide information about their program activities--kinds of programs offered, frequency, attendance. They were also asked to rate the success of each program in relation to its goals. Programs were to be interpreted in a broad sense, that is any formal effort on the part of the libraries to interact with their communities. All programs held at or by branches were included. Most of the libraries could not articulate goals of specific programs. Also, many institutions did not keep attendance records. The programs were divided into two categories--"public at large" and "community-outreach."

Public at Large. These are programs directed toward the general community, including popular films, exhibits, book talks or concerts. Also included in this category are programs devoted to health, consumer economics, politics and family topics.

The sample libraries and their branches sponsored 205 of these programs within a six-month period. Of these 205 events, 39 specific types could be identified as shown in Table 5. The "other" category consists mostly of format combinations such as film and book talk, exhibit and film, lecture and exhibit, or film and lecture.

TABLE 5

Major Types of Library Sponsored Programs

Type of Program	Number of Events	%
Films	70	34.1
Exhibits	28	13.6
Lectures	20	9.7
Concerts	8	3.9
Book Talks	7	3.4
Lecture & Discussion	6	2.9
Workshop	4	2.0
Seminar	4	2.0
Bibliography	4	2.0
Radio Show	4	2.0
Other		
Types	27	
Events	50	24.4
Total Types	37	
Total Events	205	100.0

Films accounted for more than one-third of all events held and most were directed toward no specific topic. "Weekly film night" was the most common event listed. The exhibits were usually one-man shows by local artists or local history displays. Art and investments were common lecture topics. About a third of the libraries sponsored "great books" discussion groups. The "other" category included art and poetry contests, panel discussions on abortion, meet-the-author parties and a health-food-tasting party.

Community-Outreach Programs. These were events aimed toward special groups characterized by age, education, ethnic origin, occupation, physical or mental disability. In all, 21 separate groups were identified as those likely to be found in most communities. The libraries were to provide information on all programs held at the main library and all branches within the preceeding year.

The Community-Outreach programs revealed some interesting patterns in the groups served as shown in Table 6. Programs for children represented 29.8 percent of all events for special groups. Programs designed

TABLE 6

DISTRIBUTION OF COMMUNITY-OUTREACH PROGRAMS

	Ethnic Groups	Children	Young Adults	Aged	Women's Groups	Men's Groups	Foreign Language	Incarcerated	Hospitalized	Shut-Ins	Physically Handicapped	Mentally Handicapped	Business	Labor	Disadvantaged	Illiterate	Gov't Agencies & Officials	Adult Education	Church Groups	Private Welfare Agencies	Other Groups	TOTAL
00	2	5	2						1	1			1									12
11	3	6	15	1	5			3	2						5			1	4			45
12	3	8	5	4	2	1			5	1	4		1		9			9	6	1		59
13		19	8	5																		32
14	2	2		4			3	2	1		1										1	16
15	1	12	3	3	4	1		2	1	1	1		1		4		1	3	2			34
16	4	7	1	1	1		1	1	2	2	1		5		1			1	1		3	34
17		11	2	4	1			1	1	1	2				2	1		1			1	30
18	1	9	1	5				1	1		2											21
21		2		2					1	1		1								1		10
22		12						1	3	2		1										12
24		10	3	2	2	1		1	1	1	2		3		1	1		2				26
26	1		3	1					1		1				1							12
31		4		1																		9
32		9		1				1	1		2				1			2				17
33																						0
34																			1			1
35																						0
36		2	3	3					1													8
37	1	3	3	2	5	1	1	1		2		1	1		3			1	4			28
TOTAL	18	121	46	39	20	4	5	13	22	12	16	3	12	0	27	2	1	20	18	2	5	406

for young people and the aged constituted 11.3 percent and 9.6 percent respectively of the total. Together these three groups accounted for over half (50.7%) of all programs aimed at specific populations. Programs for what might be considered power groups in a community--labor, government officials, men's clubs--were virtually non-existant.

Story hours and films were the most common types of program. Each represented 58 events or 14.3 percent of the 406 events held. Story-hours accounted for 48 percent of all children's programs. Programs for the aged, incarcerated and hospitalized were primarily provision of materials via delivery service; although a few of the libraries showed films at housing projects for older citizens. The most innovative programs were designed for children. These included arts and crafts demonstrations ranging from making model airplanes to Russian Easter eggs, folk dance lessons, and theatricals.

These data indicate:

1. That some libraries are doing considerably more than others in reaching out to their communities.
2. That certain groups receive considerably more attention in terms of special programs than others.
3. That films represent the major type of program offering over-all but that certain program formats predominate for special groups; storyhours for children, and delivery services for those who have difficulty getting to the library.
4. There seems to be no unity in programs aimed at special groups. Ruth Warncke has characterized such programs as cafeteria offerings.[4] We concur with that observation.

Two pieces of the study remain unanalyzed at this time. These are outlined below.

Library Information Questionnaire. Each library was asked to supply extensive and detailed statistical information regarding:

1. Holdings of various types of materials
2. Circulation
3. Physical plant
4. Budget allocation
5. Apportionment of staff time
6. System activities

We asked for this information for a five-year period (1966-1970). This time-span would allow any one year anomalies to be averaged out. Our purpose in collecting these data was to assess how closely these statistics matched the library's performance on the measurement criteria.

Staff Questionnaire. Every employee in the library filled out this questionnaire. The questionnaire was adapted from The Human Organization by Rensis Likert and used with the permission of McGraw Hill, the publisher.[5] The questionnaire is designed to measure the organizational atmosphere on a scale from participatory to authoritarian. We hypothesized that the way in which the staff views the organization influences the services which the library provides. We plan to correlate these staff attitudes with the other measurement indicators.

NOTES

1/   Rutgers University. Graduate School of Library Service.
Bureau of Library and Information Science Research. <u>Instruction Manual
for the Collection of Selected Public Library Information</u> (Bureau of
Library and Information Science Research, n.d.).

2/   Ernest R. De Prospo. "The Real World of the Public Library."
Speech delivered at CLEEP Conference, Wingspead, Wisconsin, April 2,
1973.

3/   Ralph U. Blasingame, Jayne L. Hess and Robert J. Bonner, <u>The
Book Collections in the Public Libraries of the Pottsville Library
District: A Date and Subject Distribution Study</u> (Pottsville Free
Public Library, 1967).

4/   Ruth Warncke, "Library Objectives and Community Needs,"
<u>Library Trends</u>, 17:6-13, 1968, p. 12.

5/   Rensis Likert, <u>The Human Organization</u> (McGraw Hill, 1967).

5. Interpreting a Library's Profile from a Management Point of View

One of the major purposes for collecting data about a library's services and operations is to provide administrators with a basis for decision-making. The facsimile computer print-out on the following pages is an example of one of the profiles given to the libraries participating in this study. The accompanying explanation is designed to illustrate how an administrator might intepret this selected data from a management viewpoint. Some caveats are in order:

1. Since the intent of this analysis is to cast detailed quantitative data into layman's terms, some generalizations about the numbers will be necessary to prevent emphasizing minutiae at the expense of the whole picture.
2. These data were collected during three days in a single week. The specific days were chosen by the libraries to represent light, medium and heavy use of the building. One might argue that these days reflect atypical use for an individual library. That may be true in some cases. However, if one compares the information for the other libraries in the same category, the data for this library is not inconsistent with the group profile.
3. The data given in the print-out represents only a portion of the information collected.
4. This particular profile was chosen randomly from the 20 in our files. The library to which the profile refers is classed as "medium-sized" having a budget over $300,000.

The facsimile print-out gives specific data for the single library being analyzed and general information for all libraries in the sample. Since these quantitative data will be discussed in general terms, it will be necessary to refer to the print-out for exact numerical information.

This analysis concentrates on three major areas: collection availability, users, and activity level. Although each of these sections provides detailed numerical data, any meaningful interpretation requires integration of the parts to understand the whole. Therefore, in some cases it will be necessary to refer to various parts of the print-out to understand the elements influencing the findings.

The column, "Your Library" gives the scores for this particular institution. To compare this library with the midpoint (average) for others of similar size, check the medium-size column under "All Phase II Libraries Median." The range columns give the lowest and highest numbers for each particular budget class.

REPORT TO LIBRARIES PARTICIPATING IN THE P.L.A. MEASUREMENT STUDY

Name of Library: Library 00

Size Category: Medium

I. Description of Collection

A. "BPR" Probability Sample

The purpose of the BPR probability sample was to determine the probability of a user obtaining any book published in the last five years. The following are the results for your library:

	Your Library	All Phase II Libraries			Low-High Range		
		Large	Median Medium	Small	Large	Medium	Small
1. Total Sample (N=500)							
a. Probability of ownership	.160	.367	.230	.122	.136-.580	.160-.288	.076-.176
b. Probability of availability	.088	.268	.180	.080	.110-.414	.088-.202	.044-.124
c. Availability of books owned	.550	.696	.720	.666	.561-.810	.550-.789	.579-.750
2. Adult Books (N=447)							
a. Probability of ownership	.143	.405	.246	.125	.181-.893	.143-.266	.076-.183
b. Probability of availability	.074	.237	.174	.083	.121-.438	.074-.192	.045-.128
c. Availability of books owned	.516	.691	.780	.661	.353-.729	.516-.967	.588-.774
3. Juvenile Books (N=53)							
a. Probability of ownership	.302	.453	.302	.075	.038-.755	.038-.472	.018-.283
b. Probability of availability	.208	.230	.226	.057	.019-.396	.019-.302	.019-.189
c. Availability of books owned	.688	.592	.688	.750	.400-.840	.500-.800	.500-1.00

B. Periodical Sample (N=80)

The periodical probability sample was drawn to determine the availability of articles listed in eight common indexes. The following are the results for your library:

	Your Library	Large	Median Medium	Small	Large	Medium	Small
1. Probability of ownership	.225	.450	.325	.188	.175-.950	.255-.450	.100-.263
2. Probability of availability	.225	.450	.313	.175	.163-.950	.188-.600	.088-.513
3. Availability of articles owned	1.00	.977	.962	.875	.895-1.00	.682-1.00	.625-1.00

C. Title Availability Sample

The title availability sample was the sample that you took of your own collection. The purpose of this sample was to be able to describe your collection as well as to determine the availability of the books that you actually own. The following are the results for your library:

	Your Library	Large	Median Medium	Small	Large	Medium	Small
1. Total Availability (N=468)	.630	.756	.818	.646	.585-.849	.630-.889	.582-.850
2. Adult Availability (N=385)	.660	.744	.846	.732	.634-.882	.660-.899	.605-.929
3. Juvenile Availability (N= 83)	.494	.636	.692	.648	.388-.846	.494-.724	.543-.746

II. Building Usage

	Your Library #	Your Library %	Median % Large	Median % Medium	Median % Small	Low-High Range Large	Low-High Range Medium	Low-High Range Small
A. Description of Users								
1. Sex								
Male	794	51.5	60.3	44.8	44.5	43.0-66.0	42.2-51.5	36.1-53.8
Female	695	45.1	38.2	52.4	54.6	30.1-53.3	45.1-55.8	44.6-62.8
No Response	53	3.4	3.2	2.8	1.6	2.2-6.9	2.0-5.5	0.9-2.4
TOTAL	1542	100.0						
2. Student-Nonstudent								
Student	730	47.3	36.1	47.3	52.7	28.4-45.1	45.1-52.6	42.8-57.1
Nonstudent	812	52.7	60.8	48.2	45.7	52.7-69.0	40.7-54.9	42.9-57.2
No Response	*	*	*	*	*	0.0-11.0	0.0-7.5	0.0-7.2
TOTAL	1542	100.0						
3. Grade Level of Students								
Elementary (K-6)	170	23.3	8.8	25.1	31.3	3.6-20.4	20.1-35.5	13.5-46.1
Junior High School (7-9)	166	22.7	14.2	19.0	19.7	2.4-25.5	12.8-22.7	13.8-22.9
High School (10-12)	212	29.0	34.9	29.7	28.0	22.3-43.9	21.5-35.1	24.1-37.1
College	116	15.9	30.2	16.7	13.5	11.6-41.6	10.7-20.9	6.2-24.5
Graduate School	6	0.8	4.1	1.9	0.4	2.1-16.8	0.2-2.4	0.0-3.4
No Response	60	8.2	6.7	6.5	6.3	3.7-20.4	4.1-9.6	0.8-12.2
TOTAL	730	100.0						
4. Occupation of Nonstudents								
Professional	138	17.0	27.0	18.1	18.7	15.3-33.2	17.0-23.3	12.6-28.1
Other White Collar	154	19.0	29.8	21.9	18.3	10.0-36.0	19.0-30.2	14.7-25.2
Blue Collar	134	16.5	15.0	10.8	10.9	5.7-17.2	8.7-16.5	6.1-16.7
Housewife/mother	121	14.9	7.7	22.5	32.2	2.5-29.8	13.8-29.5	17.1-43.3
Retired	85	10.5	9.0	9.8	6.6	5.3-15.4	1.3-10.5	1.6-15.5
Unemployed	9	1.1	3.0	1.7	1.3	0.7-6.4	1.1-2.9	0.0-3.2
No Response	171	21.0	6.3	15.9	7.6	0.5-36.9	4.6-21.0	0.4-20.7
TOTAL	812	100.0						
B. Time Entered								
9:00-9:59	121	7.8	6.9	7.8	6.3	4.2-8.6	0.1-10.5	0.0-7.3
10:00-10:59	169	11.0	7.3	9.9	5.5	5.4-8.9	7.0-11.0	4.1-7.7
11:00-11:59	143	9.3	8.3	8.7	6.0	5.8-9.5	4.4-11.0	3.0-9.1
12:00-12:59	163	10.6	11.5	9.8	6.0	7.5-15.3	5.7-13.4	2.8-11.9
1:00-1:59	200	13.0	10.4	7.4	8.9	6.5-12.5	6.9-13.0	4.5-16.1
2:00-2:59	170	11.0	8.5	10.3	6.8	6.8-10.8	6.6-11.4	2.5-14.1
3:00-3:59	168	10.9	10.1	10.4	11.2	9.4-12.6	5.7-12.7	7.4-24.7
4:00-4:59	88	5.7	8.6	6.5	11.5	7.1-10.0	3.3-9.9	8.5-15.0
5:00-5:59	51	3.3	6.5	5.8	6.9	4.7-8.5	3.9-10.0	3.6-9.9
6:00-6:59	89	5.8	7.5	9.0	10.1	5.5-10.0	2.5-8.8	5.0-15.2
7:00-7:59	120	7.8	4.5	5.1	14.4	2.5-5.8		7.0-16.8
8:00-8:59	58	3.8	0.1	0.1	7.1	0.0-2.4	0.0-0.3	4.0-8.1
No Response	2	0.1			*			0.0-1.0
TOTAL	1542	100.0						
C. Satisfaction								
Satisfied	1078	69.9	66.6	69.9	72.1	58.6-73.1	66.3-73.9	62.5-77.5
Partially Satisfied	235	15.2	18.3	16.2	16.9	8.3-20.8	15.2-21.1	13.1-22.7
Not Satisfied	138	8.9	7.1	8.0	6.7	5.7-25.8	6.1-9.4	5.0-8.6
No Response	91	6.0	6.6	4.2	5.5	3.9-20.4	3.2-6.1	2.4-9.0
TOTAL	1542	100.0						

III. Circulation

A. In-Library Circulation

In-Library circulation deals with the use of materials within the library by the patrons. The following table gives a breakdown of the types of materials used within your library and the frequency with which they were used during the three days studied.

Type of Material	Your Library #	Your Library %	All Phase II Libraries Median % Large	Medium	Small	Low-High Range Large	Medium	Small
Circulating Non-Fiction	88	28.7	26.7	25.9	21.7	12.5-36.9	10.9-48.5	17.4-40.7
Periodicals	105	34.2	26.1	28.7	25.0	9.1-33.7	24.5-34.3	18.0-31.5
General Encyclopedias	13	4.2	2.4	4.3	11.5	0.9-7.7	2.7- 9.6	5.8-41.7
Newspapers	14	4.6	10.0	7.6	4.9	0.5-23.8	0.5-18.4	0.7-22.5
Reference Books	38	12.4	14.6	12.4	10.6	4.4-23.6	3.4-30.2	4.7-15.1
Microfilm	10	3.3	4.9	0.7	*	0.8- 0.6	0.0- 3.3	0.0- 1.0
Circulating Fiction	35	11.4	4.4	1.3	6.4	2.0-15.7	0.2-26.4	0.9-17.2
Vertical File	2	0.7	2.3	0.7	4.8	0.2-11.9	0.6-11.9	0.0-22.7
Records	*		2.2	*	0.5	0.0-5.7	0.0- 0.5	0.0- 2.6
Other	2	0.7	7.0	2.6	4.4	3.2-19.6	0.7-13.4	1.3-11.5
TOTAL	307	100.0						

B. Outside the Library Circulation

Outside the library circulation deals with traditional circulation figures. The following is a breakdown of the circulation in your library during the three days studied.

	Your Library	Median Large	Medium	Small	Low-High Range Large	Medium	Small
# of Items Circulated	1404	3695	3368	1394	1379-10034	1404-4252	1033-2245
# of Users Circulating Books	451	1365	918	616	503-3410	451-1347	322- 708
Average # of Items Per User	3.12	2.89	3.12	3.23	2.56-3.89	3.10-3.67	2.95-3.30
% Users Checking Out Books	29.2%	33.8%	47.6%	38.0%	20.7-52.4	29.2-51.3	29.3-50.2

C. Items Circulated and Returned

"Items Circulated and Returned" refers to the types of items circulated. The following is a breakdown of the items that your library circulated on the three days studied.

Circulated

	Your Library #	Your Library %	Median Large	Medium	Small	Low-High Range Large	Medium	Small
Books	1491	98.5	88.5	94.2	95.3	81.2-94.0	84.5-96.0	72.5-95.8
Periodicals	*	*	*	3.0	1.0	0.0- 0.3	0.0- 3.3	0.1- 5.2
Records	21	1.4	5.2	2.4	3.4	0.0- 7.0	0.4- 4.4	2.3- 3.7
Other	1	0.1	5.0	1.0	1.9	1.2-14.5	0.0- 2.8	0.7-21.9
TOTAL	1513	100.0						

Returned:

	Your Library #	Your Library %	Median Large	Medium	Small	Low-High Range Large	Medium	Small
Books	1514	98.4	85.2	94.5	91.7	73.0-91.7	84.0-98.4	73.5-95.8
Periodicals	*	*	*	2.9	1.8	0.0- 1.6	0.0- 6.3	0.1- 4.8
Records	13	1.2	7.8	1.6	2.7	5.3-13.0	1.2- 4.5	2.4- 4.5
Other	6	0.4	7.7	1.2	1.1	0.3-16.3	0.4- 5.2	0.0-21.4
TOTAL	1538	100.0						

IV. Patterns of Reference Usage

"Patterns of Reference Usage" deals with the data that your library collected on all reference questions asked over the three day period studied. The following are the results for your library.

A. Reference Activity by Time of Day

	Your Library		All Phase II Libraries Median %			Low-High Range		
	#	%	Large	Medium	Small	Large	Medium	Small
9:00-9:59	16	5.8	6.7	4.2	3.1	5.5- 8.2	0.5- 9.3	0.6-11.8
10:00-10:59	15	5.5	8.3	9.7	4.8	7.1-19.5	5.5-13.4	2.4-10.5
11:00-11:59	24	8.7	9.1	7.9	7.8	6.6-11.6	4.3- 9.0	4.3-11.2
12:00-12:59	24	8.7	9.9	7.3	8.9	6.6-11.6	5.8-12.4	3.1-11.8
1:00-1:59	51	18.6	9.9	7.9	8.4	6.9-12.4	7.2-18.6	5.6-14.6
2:00-2:59	39	14.2	9.1	9.9	6.1	6.7-11.3	4.8-14.2	3.5-16.7
3:00-3:59	29	10.5	9.2	10.5	8.6	8.5-11.5	7.5-13.1	6.8-18.3
4:00-4:59	25	9.1	10.2	12.4	10.8	8.5-16.5	9.1-13.2	8.3-18.3
5:00-5:59	3	1.1	7.6	6.1	6.3	6.1- 8.6	1.1-10.0	4.7-10.4
6:00-6:59	16	5.8	6.2	6.5	10.6	4.3- 7.6	3.7- 8.3	3.9-12.9
7:00-7:59	24	8.7	5.5	8.7	8.2	2.8- 8.6	4.5- 9.7	4.3-15.2
8:00-8:59	9	3.3	5.0	8.6	6.8	3.4- 6.9	3.3-12.6	5.2-12.2
TOTAL	275	100.0						

B. Type of Question

	Your Library		All Phase II Libraries Median %			Low-High Range		
	#	%	Large	Medium	Small	Large	Medium	Small
Source Related	94	34.2	38.8	34.2	46.8	29.2-50.4	31.3-72.2	19.6-90.2
Directional	181	65.8	61.2	65.8	53.2	49.6-70.8	27.8-68.7	9.8-80.4
TOTAL	275	100.0						

C. Source Related Questions

1. Questionner

	Your Library		All Phase II Libraries Median %			Low-High Range		
	#	%	Large	Medium	Small	Large	Medium	Small
Student	37	39.4	22.9	46.5	44.5	15.5-34.4	39.4-61.4	28.6-63.5
Nonstudent	55	58.5	76.1	51.8	51.6	50.6-82.3	33.3-58.5	35.5-71.4
Another Library	2	2.1	2.3	1.7	*	0.0- 3.9	0.0- 3.3	0.0- 1.2
No Response	*	*	*	*	*	0.0-17.9	0.0- 2.0	0.0- 3.9
TOTAL	94	100.0						

2. Means

	Your Library		All Phase II Libraries Median %			Low-High Range		
	#	%	Large	Medium	Small	Large	Medium	Small
In Person	72	76.6	53.5	81.5	80.0	39.2-77.7	76.6-91.1	61.4-95.8
By Phone	22	23.4	46.5	18.5	16.1	22.3-60.8	8.9-23.4	4.2-38.6
No Response	*	*	*	*	*	0.0-17.9	0.0- 5.2	0.0- 3.9
TOTAL	94	100.0						

3. Searcher

	Your Library		All Phase II Libraries Median %			Low-High Range		
	#	%	Large	Medium	Small	Large	Medium	Small
Librarian	82	87.2	88.0	87.2	92.0	73.4-95.6	39.3-91.0	55.6-100.0
User	8	8.5	8.5	8.5	5.7	0.4-11.8	3.3-50.6	0.0-34.1
Both	4	4.3	1.3	4.3	5.7	0.6-10.9	1.1-14.1	0.0-24.7
No Response	*	*	0.4	0.0	0.0	0.0- 9.8	0.0- 8.9	0.0-10.3
TOTAL	94	100.0						

4. Disposition of Question

	Your Library		All Phase II Libraries Median %			Low-High Range		
	#	%	Large	Medium	Small	Large	Medium	Small
Answered	91	96.8	98.6	97.8	100.0	95.2-99.6	96.4-100.0	93.6-100.0
Referred	*	*	0.6	0.5	0.0	0.0- 3.3	0.0- 3.1	0.0- 3.2
Not Answered	3	3.2	0.7	0.5	0.0	0.3- 2.9	0.0- 3.2	0.0- 3.2
TOTAL	94	100.0						

5. Source Used to Answer Questions

	Your Library		All Phase II Libraries Median %			Low-High Range		
	#	%	Large	Medium	Small	Large	Medium	Small
Reference Book	14	14.9	24.5	21.2	20.6	13.3-34.2	14.9-32.8	12.3-31.8
Circulating Collection	10	10.6	13.4	30.4	27.3	4.5-46.6	10.6-40.0	6.8-46.6
Card Catalog	28	29.8	17.3	12.1	19.8	12.4-21.1	6.7-29.8	0.0-49.4
Index	3	3.2	9.1	6.5	5.3	3.0-13.3	2.8-11.7	2.7-19.1
Telephone Book	4	4.2	5.1	0.4	0.0	0.6-10.4	0.0-4.2	0.0-1.7
City Directory	1	1.1	3.2	0.5	0.0	0.3-9.6	0.0-3.1	0.0-2.4
Vertical File	1	1.1	3.8	1.9	3.0	1.0-7.8	0.0-7.8	0.0-9.7
Other	33	35.1	20.5	16.3	15.7	9.4-17.2	10.1-35.1	3.9-35.2
TOTAL	94	100.0						

V. Facilities Usage

Facilities Usage deals with the use of equipment and special facilities in your library by your patrons. The figures below indicate the highest incidence of use of each of the listed items during the three days that you collected this information as well as the time of day when this occured.

Type of Item	Your Library Time	All Phase II Libraries Median			Low-High Range		
	Time	Large	Medium	Small	Large	Medium	Small
Table Seating	2:30	85	57	49	2-178	2-82	0-118
Lounge Chairs & Couches	11:30	23	11	10	0-56	0-25	0-15
Photocopier	12:30	5	4	2	0-7	0-5	0-3
Meeting Room	7:30	96	77	61	0-218	0-215	0-121
Microfilm Reader (Printer)	11:30	6	2	2	0-10	0-3	0-4
Record Player	11:30	4	2	2	0-8	0-2	0-4

VI. Public Service Personnel

Public service personnel are those employees of the library that have contact with the users. The following is a profile of these individuals in your library.

	Your Library	All Phase II Libraries Median			Low-High Range		
		Large	Medium	Small	Large	Medium	Small
A. Median Age	48	33	48	45	25-48	28-48	28-53
B. Average Length of Employment In Your Library	5	7	7	7	6-11	5-10	3-13
C. Average Hours per Week at Public Service	18	18	22	19	13-21	14-24	11-36
D. Average Hours per week at Other Duties	17	17	17	17	9-23	13-24	10-25

Library 00

E. Highest Degree Earned

	Your Library		All Phase II Libraries Median			Low-High Range		
	#	%	Large	Medium	Small	Large	Medium	Small
High School	*	*	7.4	0.0	22.9	0.0-14.7	0.0-29.4	0.0-33.3
Some College	3	37.5	14.4	21.4	32.0	3.5-32.8	0.0-37.5	11.1-75.0
BA	2	25.0	28.4	35.8	25.0	15.6-50.0	5.9-50.0	11.1-27.3
MA	3	37.5	47.3	37.5	23.6	20.0-55.3	21.4-53.8	0.0-77.8
PhD	*	*	*	*	*	0.0-3.5	0.0-0.0	0.0-0.0
No Response	*	*	1.3	*	*	0.0-3.8	0.0-11.7	0.0-9.1
TOTAL	8	100.0						

F. Scheduling By Hour (Average # of People Assigned to Public Service)

	Your Library	Large	Medium	Small	Large	Medium	Small
9:00-9:59	4	10	4	2	4-26	2-10	0-7
10:00-10:59	3	11	6	3	3-31	3-10	2-7
11:00-11:59	4	11	6	3	3-31	4-10	2-7
12:00-12:59	3	10	5	3	3-28	3-8	2-5
1:00-1:59	3	11	4	3	3-27	3-9	3-6
2:00-2:59	5	12	5	4	3-33	4-11	3-7
3:00-3:59	4	11	6	5	4-34	4-11	4-9
4:00-4:59	5	12	6	4	4-31	4-10	4-9
5:00-5:59	2	14	4	4	3-26	2-8	3-6
6:00-6:59	3	8	4	5	3-17	2-6	3-5
7:00-7:59	4	7	4	5	3-19	2-6	3-5
8:00-8:59	3	7	3	5	3-18	2-6	3-5
9:00-9:59	*	5	1	0	0-12	0-2	0-5

Provision of Materials

"BPR" Probability Sample. The first score for this library is 0.16.
That means the library owns approximately 16 percent of the titles listed
in American Book Publishing Record for the past five years. However, the
average score for libraries in this budget class was 23 percent. (The
average for large libraries was 0.367 and 0.122 for small.) The range
shows the lowest and highest numbers in each budget class. Since 0.16
represents the lowest score for medium-sized libraries this institution
is at the bottom of the sample in its ownership of BPR titles.
The "Availability of Books Owned" figure represents the probability
that an owned BPR book will be on the shelf. Therefore, of the 16 percent of the BPR titles which the library holds, only slightly more than
half are available. This figure, 0.55, represents the low point for
libraries in this class.
If both ownership and shelf availability are considered--"Probability of Availability," a patron in this library has roughly nine chances
in 100 of obtaining any title listed in the BPR sample.
However, patrons who wish to obtain newer juvenile books have a
better chance of "success" in terms of both ownership and shelf availability than do those persons who want recent adult titles.
This library is at the bottom of the medium-sized library range in
its ability to supply titles from the entire BPR sample and for recent
adult titles. However, it is at the midpoint of the medium-sized class
in its ownership of BPR juvenile titles and the on-shelf availability of
these juvenile titles.
Periodical Sample. This library owns about 23 percent of the sample
periodical articles listed in common indexes. Naturally, it does not own
the same proportion of titles in each index. Every title owned is available. The library is at the bottom of the range for its class in periodical ownership.
Title Availability. A patron wishing to obtain a book which is
already in this library's collection has a 0.63 chance of finding it on
the shelves--a score nearly 20 percent below that of the average medium-
sized library. Adult books are about 17 percent more likely to be
available than juvenile books. This library is at the bottom of the medium class in the shelf availability of both adult and juvenile titles
in its collection.

Users

During the three-day period 1,542 persons entered this building.
Over half of these patrons were men. In fact, this library had a greater
percentage of male clientele than any other medium-sized library. The
average for this group was about 45 percent.
Most of the patrons (52.7 percent) are not students. They are
relatively evenly divided among the various occupational groups, with
the exception of the unemployed. However, since unemployed persons constitute a relatively small proportion of the total population, the low
figure is not unexpected.
Yet, if one compares the clientele in this library with others in
its class, significant differences emerge. This library attracts the

smallest proportion of professional and white collar workers, 36 percent versus a 40 percent average, but the highest proportion of blue collar workers and retired persons, 27 percent to 20.6 percent.

It is interesting that even though this library is at or near the bottom in the provision of materials, its users say they are as well satisfied as users of the other libraries.

Activity Level

A library's activity level is a relatively good indicator of its performance. Activity level includes the number of persons in the building, total circulation, use of facilities and the number of reference questions asked; phone questions are included.

Although attendance for the three-day study was over 1,500 it is puzzling as to just what these people do once they arrive. Only 451 (29 percent) actually borrowed any books. Nor do many of them appear to use materials in the building; only 307 in-library circulations were recorded. Nor do many of them come to attend meetings, films or other programs. The highest use of the meeting room in three days accounted for only 19 people. Reference activity is not particularly high--275 questions in three days. Even then, only 94 (34 percent) were source related. However, this percentage represents the average for medium libraries.

One might assume that staffing patterns for public service personnel would coincide with the level of activity in the building. Yet, in this particular library, there is little relationship between available staff and patrons' activity. Use of this library is concentrated between 9 a.m. and 4 p.m. Attendance falls off sharply after 4 p.m., especially in comparison with the other libraries in the medium class. The peak period for use of the building and reference is between one and two p.m., but two of the five staff members are not on duty during this hour.

This library demonstrates a markedly different pattern from others in the sample with regard to the sources used to answer reference questions. Thirty-five percent of all questions fell into the miscellaneous "other" category--nearly double the median for libraries of this size. Use of the card catalog to answer questions in this library was far above the average. But in the use of reference books and the circulating collection, this library was lowest in its category.

One might hypothesize from these data that the collection is inadequate, but the staff reported that only 3 of 91 questions could not be answered. These unanswered questions were not referred to another library. These findings suggest that there are few challenging reference questions posed in this library or that a minimal level of reference assistance is provided.

An even more serious question concerning reference service is the relationship between number and kinds of reference questions and number of hours of staff time. Taking the data from this particular library, one can analyze reference activity and staffing in the following manner.

Total hours of public service staff per day   =   43

```
Total questions asked of public service staff
     in three days                                    = 275
Average number of questions per day:  275/3           =  91.6
Number of questions per hour of public service
     staff time per day:  91.6/43                     =   2.1
```

It is conceded that there is no universally accepted definition of what constitutes a reference question. However, for purposes of this study the distinction was made between source-related questions, i.e., those requiring the use of library materials, and directional or informational questions about library hours, shelving locations and telling the patron to check the card catalog.

The calculations shown above include all types of questions. If only source-related questions are considered, the number of questions per hour of public service staff time drops sharply.

```
Total source related questions                        = 94
Average number of source related questions
     per day:  94/3                                    = 31.3
Number of source-related questions per hour
     of public service staff time per day:  31.3/43    =  0.73
```

It should be noted that the reference calculation includes only hours spent at public service desks. Therefore, the number of questions figure is not distorted by including total working hours or time spent "off the floor." However, this figure does not include total reference activity carried out in this library. Obviously some patrons are able to do their own work unassisted while others need the services of the reference staff.

Considering the fact that this library employs three persons holding masters degrees and two having the B.A., one could question both the total workload and the amount of meaningful information service these people are called upon to provide.

Table 7 summarizes how the library stands in relation to others on the sample of similar size.

TABLE 7

Comparison of this Library with Others in the "Medium" Group

ITEM	GROUP STATUS

Collection

"BPR" Probability Sample	lowest
Periodical Sample	
ownership	lowest
shelf availability	low
Title Availability	lowest

TABLE 7 (continued)

ITEM	GROUP STATUS

Users

Men	highest
Women	lowest
Student use	low
Non-student use	high
Professional workers	lowest
White collar workers	lowest
Blue collar workers	highest
Housewives	low
Retired	highest
Unemployed	lowest
User Satisfaction	median

Activity Level

Percent of users checking out materials	lowest
Percent of source related questions	median
Percent of questions asked by students	lowest
Percent of questions asked by non-students	highest
Percent of telephoned questions	highest
Total daily of staff hours for public service	low

How might an administrator use the findings to improve library service? Obviously, more money is needed to expand the book and periodical collections. But before additional funding is requested, some other measures seem appropriate.

1. Since only 29 percent of persons entering the building actually check out materials for home use and since in-library use of materials is also low, only about 100 items per day, an investigation might be made as to whether the collection actually meets the reading interests of the clientele.
2. Reduce the reference staff by one professional and use that salary to buy more books and periodicals thus increasing users' success in obtaining materials.
3. Redistribute public service staffing patterns in relation to the peak hours of building use and reference activity.

This profile cannot be used in isolation to decide what should be done to improve service in this library. The judgment of the administrator who is actually on the scene is an absolute necessity. However, the profile does indicate aspects of the library's services which are not readily apparent. For that reason, we believe that the profile even in its present preliminary state is potentially a valuable tool in evaluating library performance and assisting in decision-making.

Conclusion

As a result of the first two phases of the study, the following considerations are clear: The methodology developed is appropriate to the overall objective of the study. Selected data which measure various aspects of the public library program can be collected, with minimal assistance, at the local library level. The data themselves do discriminate the performance of one public library from that of another. The data come much closer than present library statistics to meeting the demands of both the librarian and the patron for "user-oriented" indicators which are necessary if the public library is going to reflect accurately the variety of activities that it is undertaking.

The data to be tested as a result of the study so far offers several advantages over the various measurement systems used by the states:

1. The data are comparable on a regional, state, or national basis as to (a) type of major services, (b) quality factors which modify quantitative items, and (c) personnel and management quality.
2. Not all items need to be collected each year in order to maintain the integrity of the total system.
3. A profile can be set for each library. At the same time, special local factors can be added for local decision-making.
4. The data are in a form to facilitate setting up a national data bank.
5. Previous problems encountered in traditional statistical reporting systems of defining components of data categories and counting procedures have been eliminated.
6. The data can be collected locally with a minimum of time and supervision from a state or federal agency.
7. Sampling techniques are used to measure activities otherwise not considered as subject to measurement.
8. Longitudinal reviews over a period of time, half a decade to a decade, are facilitated.
9. A factor for evaluation of library management is included.

Appendix

RATIOS AND MEDIAN TESTS OF U.S.O.E.
PUBLIC LIBRARY STATISTICS

CIRCULATION/VOLUMES ADDED
(For every volume added n books circulate)

	Total=180	Large=48	Medium=61	Small=71
Mean (circulations)	39,977	37,060	49,970	41,100
Standard deviation	17,853	17,720	16,700	18,900
Range	121,455	121,460	80,000	80,340
Median	37,054	35,750	37,160	39,000
Significance level	chi square=2.0	2DF Not significant at 0.05.		

HOLDINGS/VOLUMES ADDED
(Ratio of volumes owned to volumes added)

	Total=180	Large=48	Medium=61	Small=71
Mean (volumes)	13.381	12.97	14.28	12.88
Standard deviation	6.42	5.50	7.41	6.06
Range	54.00	34.00	50.50	32.26
Median	12.42	12.37	13.40	11.38
Significance level	chi square=3.1	2DF Not significant at 0.05.		

POPULATION/VOLUMES ADDED
(One volume added for every n persons)

	Total=180	Large=48	Medium=61	Small=71
Mean (persons)	8,057	7,460	8,090	8,430
Standard deviation	4,680	3,930	5,660	4,220
Range	37,333	26,550	35,990	22,590
Median	7,023	7,180	7,320	6,840
Significance level	chi square=2.0	2DF Not significant at 0.05.		

POPULATION/SERVICE UNITS
(Average population per service unit)

	Total=180	Large=48	Medium=61	Small=71
Mean (persons)	34,070	32,100	35,010	34,600
Standard deviation	21,022	15,190	24,900	20,970
Range	113,545	64,730	110,000	96,550
Median	27,983	28,610	26,190	28,750
Significance level	chi square=2.5	2DF Not significant at 0.05.		

CIRCULATION/PRINT MATERIALS EXPENDITURES
(For every $ spent on print materials n books circulate)

	Total=180	Large=48	Medium=61	Small=71
Mean (circulations)	11.62	8.62	8.96	15.94
Standard deviation	35.76	2.79	3.82	56.76
Range	483.81	12.04	18.45	483.81
Median	8.39	8.22	8.34	8.88
Significance level	chi square=2.3	2DF Not significant.		

PRINT MATERIALS EXPENDITURES/VOLUMES ADDED
(Average cost per volume)

	Total=180	Large=48	Medium=61	Small=71
Mean (cost)	$4.63	$4.38	$4.90	$4.57
Standard deviation	1.76	1.88	1.94	1.48
Range	15.27	15.27	13.12	9.63
Median	$4.43	$4.33	$4.77	$4.36
Significance level	chi square=1.1	2DF Not significant.		

SALARIES/TOTAL EXPENDITURES
(Fraction of the budget spent on salaries)

	Total=180	Large=48	Medium=61	Small=71
Mean (percent)	59%	62%	60%	57%
Standard deviation	0.08	0.07	0.08	0.08
Range	0.432	0.318	0.394	0.393
Median	0.591	0.617	0.611	0.564
Significance level	chi square=9.6	2DF Significant at 0.01.		

PRINT MATERIAL EXPENDITURES/TOTAL EXPENDITURES
(Fraction of the budget spent on print materials)

	Total=180	Large=48	Medium=61	Small=71
Mean (percent)	18.6%	16.1%	18.7%	20.3%
Standard deviation	0.058	0.046	0.061	0.056
Range	0.420	0.198	0.353	0.384
Median	0.178	0.154	0.172	0.197
Significance level	chi square=13.8	2DF Significant at 0.01.		

PRINT MATERIALS EXPENDITURES/SALARIES
(Ratio of print material expenditures to salaries)

	Total=180	Large=48	Medium=61	Small=71
Mean (ratio)	0.329	0.267	0.327	0.373
Standard deviation	0.136	0.097	0.144	0.135
Range	0.966	0.406	0.875	0.744
Median	0.311	0.245	0.287	0.344
Significance level	chi square=10.9	2DF Significant at 0.01.		

TOTAL EXPENDITURES/POPULATION
(Expenditures per capita)

	Total=180	Large=48	Medium=61	Small=71
Mean (dollars)	$3.96	$4.33	$4.50	$3.25
Standard deviation	2.11	1.78	2.76	1.35
Range	15.15	7.47	14.99	5.86
Median	3.53	4.15	3.52	3.17
Significance level	chi square=7.2	2DF Significant at 0.05.		

SALARIES/LIBRARY STAFF
(Average salary per staff member)

	Total=180	Large=48	Medium=61	Small=71
Mean (dollars)	$4,912	$5,410	$5,000	$4,500
Standard deviation	1,073	1,020	0,960	1,050
Range	6,566	4,880	5,530	6,570
Median	4,845	5,340	4,930	4,570
Significance Level	chi square=9.6	2DF Significant at 0.01.		

PRINT MATERIALS EXPENDITURES/POPULATION
(Print materials expenditures per capita)

	Total=180	Large=48	Medium=61	Small=71
Mean (dollars)	$0.71	$0.65	$0.81	$0.65
Standard deviation	0.40	0.23	0.55	0.30
Range	3.13	1.03	3.00	1.68
Median	0.62	0.61	0.65	0.63
Significance level	chi square=1.3	2DF Not significant.		

CIRCULATION/POPULATION
(Circulation per capita)

	Total=180	Large=48	Medium=61	Small=71
Mean (circulations)	5.91	5.59	6.35	5.75
Standard deviation	3.10	2.66	3.33	3.18
Range	16.50	12.04	15.40	16.14
Median	5.24	5.03	5.35	5.20
Significance level	chi square=4.0	2DF Not significant.		

HOLDINGS/POPULATION
(Books per capita)

	Total=180	Large=48	Medium=61	Small=71
Mean (books)	1.94	1.96	2.19	1.71
Standard deviation	1.10	0.94	1.64	0.73
Range	10.50	5.24	10.09	4.04
Median	1.76	1.74	1.93	1.67
Significance level	chi square=3.8	2DF Not significant.		

POPULATION/LIBRARY STAFF
(Population per staff member)

	Total=180	Large=48	Medium=61	Small=71
Mean (persons)	2,642	2,390	2,390	3,030
Standard deviation	1,410	1,090	1,120	1,720
Range	8,693	4,450	6,040	8,440
Median	2,283	2,170	2,220	2,590
Significance level	chi square=0.7	2DF Not significant at 0.05.		

CIRCULATION/LIBRARY STAFF
(Circulations per staff member)

	Total=180	Large=48	Medium=61	Small=71
Mean (circulations)	12,822	11,580	12,600	13,850
Standard deviation	4,492	4,090	3,630	5,190
Range	24,303	23,810	21,010	23,430
Median	12,298	11,140	12,160	13,410
Significance level	chi square=9.4	2DF Significant at 0.01.		

HOLDINGS/LIBRARY STAFF
(Holdings per staff member)

	Total=180	Large=48	Medium=61	Small=71
Mean (volumes)	4,226	4,030	4,300	4,290
Standard deviation	1,359	1,210	1,480	1,350
Range	10,940	5,820	10,840	6,630
Median	4,059	3,820	4,180	4,140
Significance level	chi square=4.0	2DF Not significant at 0.05.		

VOLUMES ADDED/LIBRARY STAFF
(Volumes added per staff member)

	Total=180	Large=48	Medium=61	Small=71
Mean (volumes)	349	330	340	400
Standard deviation	123	120	130	120
Range	755	630	670	580
Median	333	320	330	370
Significance level	chi square=3.1	2DF Not significant at 0.05.		

LIBRARY STAFF/MLS STAFF
(Number of staff members per professional)

	Total=180	Large=48	Medium=61	Small=71
Mean (persons)	8.10	7.70	8.10	8.38
Standard deviation	8.06	10.26	6.17	7.91
Range	70.50	68.38	34.00	39.00
Median	5.99	5.30	6.38	6.47
Significance level	chi square=4.2	2DF Not significant at 0.05.		

POPULATION/MLS STAFF
(Population per MLS staff member)

	Total=180	Large=48	Medium=61	Small=71
Mean (persons)	22,310	19,440	19,460	26,700
Standard deviation	26,968	27,950	19,570	31,230
Range	148,000	142,310	111,000	148,000
Median	13,266	11,810	13,720	16,080
Significance level	chi square=2.9	2DF Not significant at 0.05.		

CIRCULATION/MLS STAFF

(Circulations per MLS staff member)

	Total=180	Large=48	Medium=61	Small=71
Mean (circulations)	101,189	89,420	100,090	110,090
Standard deviation	99,185	112,580	78,880	105,530
Range	668,000	651,550	360,000	464,000
Median	69,690	53,520	70,240	76,080
Significance level	chi square=2.9	2DF Not significant		

HOLDINGS/MLS STAFF

(Holdings per MLS staff member)

	Total=180	Large=48	Medium=61	Small=71
Mean (volumes)	33,961	29,590	33,880	37,000
Standard deviation	31,407	31,250	25,610	35,800
Range	187,000	179,760	140,000	166,000
Median	24,047	20,810	27,290	24,690
Significance level	chi square=7.0	2DF Significant at 0.05.		

VOLUMES ADDED/MLS STAFF

(Volumes added per MLS staff member)

	Total=180	Large=48	Medium=61	Small=71
Mean (volumes)	2,747	2,330	2,830	2,960
Standard deviation	2,676	2,550	2,620	2,810
Range	16,600	16,600	12,000	10,000
Median	2,010	1,670	2,190	2,190
Significance level	chi square=3.9	2DF Not significant at 0.05.		

CIRCULATION/HOLDINGS

(Circulations per volume owned)

	Total=180	Large=48	Medium=61	Small=71
Mean (circulations)	3,189	3,020	3,080	3,390
Standard deviation	1,149	1,130	910	1,320
Range	6,927	5,380	4,510	6,930
Median	3,062	2,930	3,010	3,240
Significance level	chi square=6.9	2DF Significant at 0.05.		

Selected Bibliography

American Library Association. Committee on Post-War Planning.
  Post-War Standards for Public Libraries. American Library Association, 1943.

American Library Association. Public Libraries Division. Co-ordina-
ting Committee on Revision of Public Library Standards.
  Public Library Service: A Guide to Evaluation with Minimum
  Standards. American Library Association, 1956.

American Library Association. Statistics Co-ordinating Project.
  Library Statistics: A Handbook of Concepts, Definitions and
  Terminology. American Library Association, 1966.

American Library Association Public Library Association. Standards
Committee.
  Minimum Standards for Public Library Systems, 1966. American
  Library Association, 1967.

Andrews, T.
  "Role of Department Libraries in Operations Research Studies
  in University Library." Special Libraries, 59:519-24, September-
  October, 1968.

Argyris, Chris.
  Interpersonal Competence and Organizational Effectiveness.
  Dorsey Press, 1962.

Beasley, Kenneth E.
  Measurement of Effectiveness of Public Library Service. Proposal
  for Research Submitted to the U.S. Commissioner of Education,
  January, 1970.

Beasley, Kenneth E.
  A Statistical Reporting System for Local Public Libraries. Pennsylvania State Library Monograph No. 3. University Park, Institute of Public Administration, The Pennsylvania State University,
  1964.

64

Beasley, Kenneth E.
"A Theoretical Framework for Public Library Measurement." In,
Illinois. University. Graduate School of Library Science.
Research Methods in Librarianship: Measurement and Evaluation.
Graduate School of Library Science, 1968.

Blasingame, Ralph U., Jayne L. Hess and Robert J. Bonner.
The Book Collections in the Public Libraries of the Pottsville
Library District: A Date and Subject Distribution Study.
Pottsville Free Public Library, 1967.

Boaz, Martha.
"Evaluation of Special Library Service for Upper Management."
Special Libraries, 59:789-91, 1968.

Boaz, R.L.
"Dilemma of Statistics for Public Libraries." ALA Bulletin,
63:1572-5, December, 1969.

Bowker, R.R., Inc.
American Library Directory. 28th ed. Bowker, 1971.

Bowker, R.R., Inc.
The Bowker Annual of Library and Book Trade Information, 1971.
Bowker, 1971.

Brown, A.L.
"Measurement of Performance and Its Relationship for Special
Library Service." Special Libraries, 50:379-84, 1959.

Buckland, M.K., et al.
Systems Analysis of a University Library. Lancaster, England,
University of Lancaster, 1970.

Bundy, M.L.
"Factors Influencing Public Library Use." Wilson Library Bulletin, 42:371-82, December, 1967.

Bundy, M.L.
"Metropolitan Public Library Use." Wilson Library Bulletin,
41:950-61, May, 1967.

Burkhalter, Barton R.
Case Studies in Systems Analysis in a University Library.
Scarecrow, 1968.

Bush, G.C., et al.
"Attendance and Use of the Science Library at M.I.T." American
Documentation, 7:87-109, 1956.

Campbell, Angus and C.A. Metzner.
Public Use of the Library and Other Sources of Information.
Univeristy of Michigan, Institute for Social Research, 1950.

Campbell, H.C.
Metropolitan Public Library Planning Throughout the World.
Pergamon, 1967.

Carnovsky, Leon.
"Evaluation of Library Services." UNESCO Bulletin for Libraries,
13:221, 1959.

Carnovsky, Leon.
"Evaluation of Public Library Facilities." In, Wilson, Louis R.
Library Trends. University of Chicago Press, 1937, pp. 286-309.

Carnovsky, Leon.
"Measurements in Library Service." In, Joeckel, Carleton B.
Current Issues in Library Administration. University of Chicago
Press, 1939, pp. 240-63.

Carnovsky, Leon.
"Public Library Surveys and Evaluation." Library Quarterly,
25:23-36, January, 1955.

Chapman, E.A., et al.
Library Systems Analysis Guidelines. Wiley-Interscience, 1970.

Chicago. University. Graduate Library School.
Operations Research: Implications for Libraries. The Thirty-
fifth Annual Conference of the Graduate Library School. Ed. by
Don R. Swanson and Abraham Bookstein. University of Chicago
Press, 1972.

Churchman, C. West.
The Systems Approach. Delta, 1968.

Clapp, Verner and Robert T. Jordan.
"Quantitative Criteria for Adequacy of Academic Library Collections." College and Research Libraries, 26:371-80, 1965.

Crowley, Terrence and Thomas A. Childers.
Information Service in Public Libraries. Scarecrow, 1971.

De Prospo, Ernest R.
"The Real World of the Public Library." Speech delivered at CLEEP
Conference, Wingspead, Wisconsin, April 2, 1973.

Dick, Elizabeth and Bernard Berelson.
"What Happens to Library-Circulated Books?" Library Quarterly,
18:100-7, 1948.

Drexel Institute of Technology.
Problems of Library Services in Metropolitan Areas. Drexel
Press, 1966.

Durham University.
Project for Evaluating the Benefits from University Libraries:
Final Report. University Computer Unit, 1969.

Evans, Charles.
Middle Class Attitudes and Public Library Use. Libraries
Unlimited, 1970.

Fussler, Herman A. and J.L. Simon.
Patterns in the Use of Books in Large Research Libraries.
University of Chicago Press, 1969.

Gardiner, G.L.
"The Empirical Study of Reference." College and Research Libraries, 30:130-55, 1969.

Gelfand, Morris A.
"Techniques of Library Evaluation in the Middle States Association." College and Research Libraries, 19:305-20, 1958.

Georgopoulous, Basil S. and Arnold S. Tannenbaum.
"A Study of Organizational Effectiveness." American Sociological
Review, 22:34-40, 1957.

Hamburg, Morris, Leonard E. Ramist and Michael R.W. Bommer.
"Library Objectives and Performance Measures and Their Use in
Decision Making." Library Quarterly, 42:107-28, 1972.

Hamburg, Morris, (Director), Richaed C. Clelland, Michael R.W. Bommer,
Leonard E. Ramist, Donald M. Whitfield.
Library Planning and Decision-Making Systems. Final Report.
U.S. Department of Health, Education, and Welfare. Bureau of
Libraries and Education Technology, December 1972.

Hamburg, Morris, et al.
A Systems Analysis of the Library and Information Science Statistical Data System. U.S. Office of Education. Bureau of Research,
1970.

Hoadley, Irene Braden and Clark, Alice S., eds.
Quantitative Methods in Librarianship. Greenwood Press, 1972.

Houser, Lloyd J.
Indices of Effectiveness of Public Library Services. Ph.D. Disser-
tation. Rutgers, 1968.

Illinois. University. Graduate School of Library Service.
     Measurement and Evaluation; Research in Librarianship. Graduate
     School of Library Service, 1968.

Institute for the Advancement of Medical Communication.
     Checklist of Library Policies on Services to Other Libraries.
     Philadelphia, 1968.

Institute for the Advancement of Medical Communication.
     Guide for Inventory of Library Policies on Services to Individual
     Users. Philadelphia, 1968.

Jain, A.K.
     "Sampling and Data Collection Methods for a Book Use Study."
     Library Quarterly, 39:245-52, 1969.

Jain, A.K.
     "Sampling and Short Period Usage in the Purdue Library." College
     and Research Libraries, 27:211-8, 1966.

Kaiser, Walter H.
     "Statistical Trends of Large Public Libraries." Library Quarter-
     ly, 18:275-81, 1948.

Knight, Douglas M. and E. Shepley Nourse.
     Libraries at Large: The Resource Book Based on the Materials of
     the National Advisory Commission on Libraries. Bowker, 1969.

Krikelas, James.
     Library Statistics and State Agencies. Illinois State Library,
     1968.

Krikelas, James.
     "Library Statistics and the Measurement of Library Services."
     ALA Bulletin, 60:494-99, 1966.

Likert, Rensis.
     The Human Organization. McGraw Hill, 1967.

Maizell, R.E.
     "Standards for Measuring the Effectiveness of Technical Library
     Performance." Institute of Radio Engineers Transactions on
     Engineering Management EM-7, 1960, pp. 69-72.

Martin, Allie Beth.
     A Strategy for Public Library Change: Proposed Public Library
     Goals-Feasibility Study. American Library Association, 1972.

Martin, Lowell.
     Library Response to Urban Change. American Library Association,
     1969.

68

Mathematica.
    On Library Statistics, Submitted to the National Advisory Commis-
    sion on Libraries. U.S. Office of Education. Bureau of Research,
    1967.

Meier, Richard L.
    "Efficiency Criteria for the Operation of Large Libraries."
    Library Quarterly, 31:215-34, 1961.

Millett, John D.
    Management in the Public Service: the Quest for Effective Per-
    formance. McGraw-Hill, 1954.

Morse, Philip M.
    Library Effectiveness. M.I.T. Press, 1968.

National Center for Education Statistics.
    Statistics of Public Libraries Serving Areas with at Least
    25,000 Inhabitants. 1968. G.P.O., 1970.

National Conference on Library Statistics, 1966. Ed. by A.F. Trezza
    and James Beasley. American Library Association, 1967.

Newhouse, Joseph P. and Alexander, Arthur J.
    An Economic Analysis of Public Library Services. Rand Corporation,
    1972.

Nie, Norman, Dale H. Brent and C. Hadlai Hull.
    SPSS: Statistical Package for the Social Sciences. McGraw-Hill,
    1970.

Olson, Edwin E.
    Survey of User Policies in Indiana Libraries and Information
    Centers. Indiana Library Studies, Report no. 10. April, 1970.

O'Neill, Edward T.
    "Sampling University Library Collections." College and Research
    Libraries, 27:450-4, 1966.

Orr, Richard H., et al.
    "Development of Methodologic Tools for Planning and Managing
    Library Services." Medical Library Association Bulletin,
    56:241-67, July 1968 and 380-403, October 1968.

Parker, E.B. and W.J. Paisley.
    "Predicting Library Circulation from Community Characteristics."
    Public Opinion Quarterly, 29:39-53, 1965.

Penna, C.V.
    "Library Inspection." UNESCO Bulletin for Libraries, 23:170-7,
    1969.

Pings, Vern M.
"Development of Quantitative Assessment of Medical Libraries."
College and Research Libraries, 29:373-80, 1968.

Pizer, Irwin L. and A.M. Cain.
"Objective Tests of Library Performance." Special Libraries,
59:704-11, 1968.

Poole, Frazier G.
"Performance Standards and Specifications in the Library Economy."
Library Trends, 11:436-44, 1963.

Raffel, Jeffrey and Robert Shishko.
Systematic Analysis of University Libraries; An Application of
Cost-Benefit Analysis to the M.I.T. Libraries. M.I.T. Press,
1969.

Rather, John Carson and Nathan M. Cohen.
Statistics of Libraries: An Annotated Bibliography of Recurring
Surveys. U.S. Office of Education, 1961.

Ridley, C.E. and H.A. Simon.
"Measuring Public Library Service." Public Management, 19:203-8,
1937.

Rockwood, Charles E. and Ruth H. Rockwood.
Quantitative Guides to Public Library Operation. Illinois.
University. Graduate School of Library Science. Occasional
Paper, 1967.

Rogers, R.B.
"Measurement and Evaluation." Library Trends, 3:177-87, 1954.

Roscoe, John T.
Fundamental Research Statistics for the Behavioral Sciences.
Holt, Reinhart and Winston, 1969.

Rosenberg, K.C.
"Evaluation of an Industrial Library." Special Libraries,
60:635-8, 1969.

Rothstein, Samuel.
"The Measurement and Evaluation of Reference Service." Library
Trends, 12:456-72, 1964.

Rutgers University. Graduate School of Library Service. Bureau of
Library and Information Science Research.
Instruction Manual for the Collection of Selected Public Library
Information. Bureau of Library and Information Science Research,
n.d.

Salverson, C.A.
  "Relevance of Statistics to Library Evaluation." College and
  Research Libraries, 30:352-61, 1969.

Schick, Frank L.
  "Coordinated Collection and Individual Use of Library Statistics."
  Library Trends, 13:117-25, 1964.

Schick, Frank L.
  "The Evaluation of Library Resources by Standards and Statistics."
  In, Castagna, Edwin. National Inventory of Library Needs.
  American Library Association, 1965.

Sewell, P.H.
  "Evaluation of Library Services in Depth." UNESCO Bulletin for
  Libraries, 22:274-80, 1968.

Slamecka, Vladimer.
  "A Selective Bibliography on Library Operations Research."
  Library Quarterly, 42:152-158, 1972.

"Standards for Libraries."
  Library Trends, 21, 1972.

Tauber, Maurice F. and Irlene Roemer Stephens, eds.
  Library Surveys. Columbia University Press, 1967.

Tauber, Maurice F.
  "Survey Method in Approaching Library Problems." Library Trends,
  13:15-30, 1964.

Thompson, John I., Co.
  Criteria for Evaluating the Effectiveness of Library Operations
  and Services. 1967-68 (ATLIS reports nos. 10, 19, 21) 3v.

Thompson, Lawrence S.
  "History of the Measurement of Library Service." Library Quarterly, 21:94-106, 1951.

Trueswell, Richard W.
  "A Quantitative Measure of User Circulation Requirements and
  Its Possible Effect on Stack Thinning and Multiple Copy Deter-
  mination." American Documentation, 16:20-5, 1965.

Trueswell, Richard W.
  "Some Behavioral Patterns of Library Users: the 80/20 Rule."
  Wilson Library Bulletin, 43:458-61, 1969.

Trueswell, Richard W.
  "User Circulation Satisfaction vs. Size of Holding at Three
  Academic Libraries." College and Research Libraries, 30:204-13,
  1969.

Warncke, Ruth.
    "Library Objectives and Community Needs." _Library Trends_,
    17:6-13, 1968.

Weiss, Carol H.
    Evaluation Research: Methods of Assessing Program Effectiveness.
    Prentice-Hall, 1972.

Wessel, C.J.
    "Criteria for Evaluating Technical Library Effectiveness."
    ASLIB Proceedings, 20:455-81, 1968.

Yenawine, Wayne S. ed.
    Library Evaluation. Syracuse University Press, 1959.